Social Skills for the Overthinker:
Beat Self-Sabotage, Escape Your Comfort Zone, and Get Out Of Your Head

by Nick Trenton

www.NickTrenton.com

Table of Contents

CHAPTER ONE: INSIDE THE OVERTHINKER'S MIND — 7

- RUMINATION — 7
- THE SPOTLIGHT EFFECT — 19
- OVERCOMING GENERALIZATION — 30

CHAPTER TWO: GETTING OUT OF YOUR HEAD — 43

- CURIOSITY IS MEDICINE — 43
- DO THE OPPOSITE — 53
- CHALLENGE YOUR INNER CRITIC — 63

CHAPTER THREE: ENGAGE AGAIN — 77

- VISUALIZATION — 77
- HOW TO USE ROLE-PLAYING — 85
- THE POWER OF RANDOM ACTS OF KINDNESS — 93

CHAPTER FOUR: TAKE ACTION! — 105

- PUT A FENCE AROUND YOUR RUMINATION — 106
- EXPOSURE THERAPY — 117
- LETTING GO OF SAFETY-SEEKING BEHAVIORS — 128
- SOCIAL EXHAUSTION — 140

CHAPTER FIVE: DEVELOPING RELAXED COMMUNICATION — 151

BULLETPROOF CONVERSATION SKILLS	**152**
TRY IMPROV	**159**
MASTERING ASSERTIVE COMMUNICATION	**170**

SUMMARY GUIDE — 183

Chapter One: Inside the Overthinker's Mind

Rumination

Meet Jaime. She is someone who "hates small talk" and has never found socializing easy. She believes that it's difficult to make friends and stressful to keep them, and frequently wonders whether it's all worth it. Why do other people seem to find it so much easier than she does? Having stewed over the problem for literally decades, she eventually concludes that it's because she's too sensitive, she's an introvert, she has low self-esteem.

But the truth is, none of these reasons are the real cause of Jaime's difficulty with people. Take a look at the following scenario and see if you can spot what the problem really is.

Jaime has just finished a Zoom meeting with colleagues and a few supervisors. It was pure hell. She finds herself lightheaded, on edge, and unable to settle down to anything for the rest of the day. For a few moments she even feels tearful and then suddenly angry. She tries to focus on her work, but she can't help returning to a moment in the meeting when she was asked a question. She replays the awkward moment in her mind over and over again. Was she too flustered? Could everyone tell she was nervous? Why did she say what she did instead of something clearer, more intelligent, smoother? Why did she have to be such an idiot and mispronounce the word "epitome"? When the supervisor remarked that it was "time to cut to the chase," was he actually referring to her? Did they all think she talked too much? Did she ramble? Was her answer really unsophisticated, or worse—did it hurt someone's feelings? Cross a line? Why was everyone quiet for a few seconds after she spoke?

Phew! Now, reading all the above, can you see that Jaime's problem is not *socializing* at all? Jaime does not have a problem with social situations or with other people. She doesn't have a problem with her work, her communication style, her appearance, her intelligence, or any of the other things her brain is feverishly throwing up as a potential threat. Rather, **Jaime's problem is that she is**

overthinking—and it's making everything worse. Jaime's particular flavor of rumination is called post-event rumination, and it's what it sounds like: painfully replaying social events in the mind over and over, but only focusing on negative aspects, or even inventing them from scratch.

In this book, we'll be looking at the phenomenon of social anxiety, but with a big focus on the *anxiety* part. There are plenty of ways to learn to communicate, to make friends, to listen well, and to build rapport. But none of these techniques can be done if you are so anxious that you cannot get out of your head long enough to start practicing them. Thus, **in solving the anxiety problem, we free ourselves up to engage with socializing for what it is: a safe, neutral skill that can be learned and mastered, just like any other skill.**

Throughout the book, we'll be examining exactly how anxiety gets in the way of us learning to develop natural, enjoyable, and spontaneous social interaction with others. As we move through each chapter, it's as though we are gradually stepping outside of our anxious rumination—and taking one step at a time out into the world to engage actively with our environment, with other people, and with the real, living present moment.

Think of it this way: **Anxiety is an act of narrowing.** Stress and tension tightens and narrows the body, the breath, the entire nervous system. It also tightens and narrows your field of awareness so that your whole world shrinks down to a small space inside your head. And that's stressful! From inside this constricted, anxious place, we are trapped and unable to connect to anything outside our awareness.

Socializing successfully with others is an act of opening up. Connecting with the outside world and everything in it requires we move away from ourselves, our habitual narratives, our preoccupations, our fears, and our fixed limits, and reach out to encounter something or someone else.

To prove this to yourself, think of the last time you felt truly socially anxious. Think back to the situation now and imagine what it was like (maybe it's like Jaime's awful Zoom meeting!). You might remember your racing heart, the queasy feeling in your stomach, the million-miles-an-hour thoughts going through your head, the awkwardness.

But do you remember looking into another person's eyes and feeling a moment of connection? Do you remember what the room looked like or what other people were wearing or what the weather was doing? What music was playing? Can you remember the tiny details of the things people told you? Chances are, you can't remember any of this, because at the time, anxiety had narrowed your perception so tightly that all you could notice was your own discomfort. As a result, you cannot honestly say you are bad at socializing . . . because you haven't actually tried it yet!

This is why we won't begin this book on overthinking with yet more overthinking (i.e., ruminating over how much we ruminate!). There is no point on dwelling in hair-splitting detail over the past and what it was and how bad it felt. We're not going to dissect your posture, your speech patterns, or your appearance, because *those things were never the problem*. Rather, we're going to take a step back and look at the way we are talking to ourselves about our behavior in the first place.

How to Stop the Cycle
First, you experience a social situation. After it ends, you start ruminating over it. "Ruminate" is a word that comes from the class of animal called ruminants—literally those that "chew the cud." You bring out a collection of awful-feeling thoughts and chew them round and

round, and they get worse and worse each time you go over them. By the time you're done chewing, you're left with a firm belief that you're terrible, that everyone hates you, and that you can't stand socializing for even a second. You take this attitude into your next social situation, and no surprise, the vicious circle starts another turn.

First, recognize that social rumination is a cycle. Why are you this way and why does your brain do this? Well, that's unimportant. Remember that "a vicious cycle has no root," so it's really irrelevant what started it initially. Instead, become curious about what is maintaining that cycle. Stop doing *that*, and the cycle stops turning.

Step 1: Admit that your evaluation is distorted

The anxious mind takes a tiny crumb of data and creates whole worlds of meaning out of it. Just pause and acknowledge that you're doing it. The person looking at you is just . . . looking at you. The conclusion that they are judging you, that they are angry, or that there must be something wrong with your face is all additional data that *you* are adding (and don't need to continue adding). In other words, just pause and notice that not everything your brain tells you is automatically one hundred percent true.

Step 2: Separate emotions from reality

In the same way that your thoughts can be distorted, so can your emotional processes. A big issue with overthinkers is the following error in reasoning:

"I felt so anxious and embarrassed after the party. I must have made a fool of myself."

Let's look closely at this. The implication seems to be that if I feel anxious, there must be a reason "out there" in the world for me to be feeling this way. It must have objectively been a stressful situation. Or, if I feel guilty or awkward, that must mean I must have done something objectively wrong.

If you have trouble understanding the difference, think of it in terms of anger. Have you ever seen someone get really annoyed with other people for no reason? Imagine someone who immediately blames someone else when they stub their toe by accident. They seem to be saying, "I'm feeling angry and hurt . . . so that means someone must have hurt me!"

Again, pause and realize that your *appraisal* of reality might not be the same as reality itself. You might have felt that an event was simply awful . . . but was it? Be clear in your naming and labeling. "I felt awful about this situation" is more accurate than "it was an awful situation."

"I was so awkward" is not quite right; it's better to say "I felt fear" or "I felt anxious." You shift your language from labeling *yourself* ("I was so awkward"; "I'm a socially awkward person") to labeling experiences: ("I felt anxious"). Ask yourself:

Am I ignoring any important aspects of the social situation?
Am I making assumptions about what other people are thinking?
Am I jumping to conclusions about what this means for my future or the relationship at hand?

Step 3: Separate discomfort from disaster

Now we're getting somewhere.

Let's be honest: Some social situations *are* a bit tricky. Maybe you do put your foot in it or fumble your words. It happens. But the way we interpret these events makes all the difference. Even if your worst fears came true and you really did say something stupid—so what? It's definitely uncomfortable, but it's not the end of the world. You'll go on living, and you're still the same person you always were, with your good and bad qualities, and life goes on.

Some theorists guess that social rejection feels so bad because our emotions evolved in a context where being rejected by your social group really did have serious consequences for survival. But we need to recognize this knee-jerk tendency and moderate it when we see it. "If my colleagues don't like me, that's it—I won't be able to cope; it will be the end for me and totally unbearable." Really? Would you really shrivel up and die from a moment of awkwardness?

We need to get skilled at noticing that there are many shades of discomfort long before truly unbearable, scary pain. Those who are good at socializing actually feel *more* unpleasant feelings than those who struggle.

When you ruminate, you may be approaching situations from this life-or-death mindset, and your brain wants to protect you from what it sees as a serious threat. But the worst that can happen is that you momentarily feel bad. That's it. You can handle momentary feelings—you can even get good at handling them!

Anxiety is not dangerous, and it's not the end of the world, either. Sometimes we ruminate because we think it's a way to avoid having to experience unpleasant feelings. Maybe we hope that somehow, we can control other people's actions toward us, or control their opinions of us, so that everything will be perfect and we'll never have to put a foot wrong or feel vulnerable. Isn't that silly when it's said out in the open like that?

Sometimes post-event rumination comes down to a big gap between how we think we ought to have behaved, and how we think we did behave. One solution: dropping the "shoulds" and being a bit kinder to ourselves. Do you expect other people to express themselves perfectly all the time? If not, then don't expect it from yourself. Another solution is to be a bit more generous in your appraisal of how you actually behaved. If a neutral third party were to look at your behavior, would they be as harsh in their interpretation as you're being?

Accept that imperfection is normal in relationships. Communication is never faultless, and a little friction is a given. Allow yourself to be a little rusty now and then, and lower the stakes—it's just an interaction, not the defining moment of your life. Shift from seeking perfection to valuing *genuine connections* with others. That means learning to embrace vulnerability. Give yourself permission to be as you are, i.e., flawed, in process, dynamic. Remind yourself that other people are in the same position as you!

How do these three steps play out in Jaime's life?

After the Zoom call, she takes some time to journal her feelings and make a plan for the next meeting (note—*not* rumination!). She takes a moment to write down a stream-of-consciousness list of all her anxious thoughts and feelings, then stops and looks at them objectively and with some distance.

- Is there any evidence for these assumptions, conclusions, and judgments?
- Are expectations and standards too high or unrealistic?
- Is there something positive in the situation that is being ignored?
- Is there some room for more self-compassion?

Slowing down in this way allows Jaime to have an astonishing insight: The Zoom call was completely, utterly unremarkable. She even returns to watch a recording of the meeting, and with neutral eyes, she can see that not only was she not behaving awkwardly, but that the conversation was productive, respectful, and interesting. She realizes that all her angst and discomfort was purely a product of her own overthinking.

The Spotlight Effect

David Foster Wallace once said, "You will worry less about what people think of you when you realize how seldom they do."

Let's return to this idea of narrowed attention. **The spotlight effect refers to a psychological phenomenon where individuals tend to overestimate how much others notice and care about their appearance or behavior in social settings—** i.e., it's this excruciating feeling of being "in the spotlight" and heavily scrutinized by others. As you can imagine, this is a cognitive distortion—it is really that *we are focusing intently on ourselves*; it is not something that others are doing to us.

This distortion leads to increased social anxiety, as people believe they are constantly being watched and appraised. However, multiple studies, including one conducted by Tom Gilovich and colleagues in 2000, have consistently shown that these perceptions are often wildly exaggerated.

In one experiment, students were asked to wear genuinely embarrassing T-shirts and estimate how many people in the room would notice. Their estimates were significantly higher than the actual number of people who took notice. Similarly, when other students watched recordings of these situations and were asked to estimate the number of people who would notice the shirt, their estimations aligned more closely with reality.

Another study involved non-embarrassing T-shirts featuring well-known figures such as Bob Marley and Martin Luther King Jr. Once again, the students wearing the shirts overestimated how many people would notice and recall the shirt. In contrast, the actual number of people who did so was significantly lower.

The key takeaway is that most individuals are primarily focused on their own lives, thoughts, and activities, leaving little attention for others' appearances or actions. The best-case scenario is that people are simply engrossed in the actual unfolding conversation, and flowing with the interaction itself, rather than getting hung up on inconsequential details. Either way, anxiety can make you feel as though you and the things you do are taking up way more space in the world than they really are. It may sound a little harsh, but try to remind yourself that nobody actually cares! The next time you're out in a public space, ask how much attention you're paying to small details of a person's appearance or behavior. Even if you do notice these things, how long does your focus on it last? And is it always accompanied by judgment and negativity? Probably not!

Here's how to turn that spotlight off.

Assess the spotlight: When you catch yourself thinking that the "negative" spotlight is on you, take a moment to evaluate whether the spotlight is actually self-imposed, i.e., it's really just you being hyper-focused on yourself.

If you catch the spotlight setting in, try to broaden its beam a little and take in more of your surroundings. Focus on something other than your own body, your sensations, your appearance, your thoughts. One excellent way to do this is to deeply focus on the other person and really listen to what they're saying. Abandon yourself and enter their world. The sense of relief can be immediate. You realize that the spotlight was your own scrutiny and not a characteristic of the situation.

Challenge baseless anxiety: Having a spotlight on you is not in itself a terrifying experience. Think about it: Simply being observed is not dangerous, unpleasant, or threatening. Instead, it's our simultaneous belief that we are being judged that makes this feeling so painful.

But again, this is usually a distortion. You can never know for sure what others are thinking (seriously, many people don't even know themselves what they're thinking!), and even if you did, you can't do a lot to control it, anyway. Recognize that people have their own concerns and are unlikely to dwell on your actions unless they directly impact them. Every person you encounter is the main character in their own story, and they inhabit a whole rich universe all their own—a universe that you likely play the tiniest role in.

Be kind to yourself: When you find yourself in a situation where social anxiety is taking over, imagine that a close friend is experiencing the same thing. Ask yourself what you would say to them to offer support and encouragement. Chances are, you wouldn't tell them a fraction of the kind of thing you tell yourself! If you catch yourself thinking, "Well, my friend is a normal person, but obviously it's different for *me* because I'm genuinely weird," then just ask yourself what you would say to a friend who told you this!

The Curse of Taking Things Personally
As you can see, there is a strange irony emerging: Those who are painfully self-conscious tend to take part in a kind of anxious self-absorption that keeps their focus always on *me me me*. The people who are relaxed in

themselves, comfortable, confident, and successful in social interactions are actually those who are thinking about themselves the least.

The spotlight effect can make us wrongly assume that we are somehow the center of things, or that everything that happens around us must in some way connect back to us and what we are doing or saying. The psychological term *personalization* refers to continually referring neutral events back to the self—for example, assuming that negative events are somehow your fault. A related cognitive distortion is mind reading, where we make quick assumptions about what other people are thinking or feeling, without a shred of evidence.

For example, someone in a group sighs and says loudly, "I'm bored!" and your immediate reaction is to think that you are not being interesting enough, and that they have leveled something of an accusation at you for not being entertaining. Or a waitress tells you, "Sorry, we don't let people make substitutions on the breakfast menu," and you interpret this to mean that she is annoyed with you personally for making a request for a substitution.

The fact is, social situations are often ambiguous. There is a lot of information flying around, and other people's intentions, motivations, thoughts, and feelings are often invisible to us. Nevertheless, we have to make a working model if we are to make sense of other people. Anxious overthinkers tend to do this in a negative, distorted, and unhelpful way. If you're faced with uncertainty about others' thoughts, anxiety can make you jump to the conclusion that *you* are the problem. It takes a little practice to notice yourself doing this and step back. Are there other things going on in the world besides you and how terrible you are?

Jokes aside, many of us have learned to personalize through past experience. Our upbringing may have wrongly taught us to accept responsibility for other people's emotions or behaviors, and we may have gotten into the habit of internalizing blame that isn't rightly ours. Later, as adults, it's as though we have a set of dominoes set up, each domino a negative, self-critical thought. An external stimulus (like someone saying "I'm bored!") sets off the chain of dominoes in an entirely automatic way.

In Jaime's case, when the supervisor said "time to cut to the chase" in the Zoom call, this set off a whole chain of thoughts and feelings in which Jaime felt that not only was the supervisor angry/annoyed (mind reading) but also that she herself was the cause for it (personalizing). The reality is very much smaller and unremarkable: Jaime's supervisor said that because he had an agenda and was aware that it was time to move to the next talking point. Pretty boring, huh?

This kind of distorted thinking can keep going, domino after domino. Jaime's rumination then starts to become:

Personal—the supervisor has an issue with her directly, and maybe even hates her.

Permanent—this is just the way things are now, and will be forever.

Pervasive—probably the other supervisors feel the same, and while she's at it, she guesses most people in her life agree and find her intolerable.

If you recognize some of this in yourself, rest assured it's easy to address.

Distinguish between Thoughts, Feelings, and Reality

First, understand the difference between feelings and thoughts. Feelings can often be summarized in one word (e.g., happy, scared), while thoughts are the ideas that drive or follow those feelings. Although you may not control uncomfortable emotions, you can choose coping strategies to respond to thinking traps effectively.

Feeling: Nervous

Thought: "My boss only said a quick "Hi!" today. I must've done something to upset him."

In this example, the feeling is nervousness, and the thought is assuming that you did something wrong. Recognizing the distinction between the feeling of nervousness and the thought about how others will perceive you can help you cope with the situation more effectively. Finally, recognize that both thought and feeling are completely distinct from the reality of the situation.

Practice Labeling

Whenever you experience emotions or thoughts, try to label them separately. Using the previous example, identify the thought behind it, such as assuming the other person doesn't like talking to you. By recognizing your tendencies to personalize or mind read, you can better understand and manage your emotional responses.

By labeling the situation, feeling, and thought, you can separate them and gain awareness of your thoughts. "I feel like he's annoyed with me . . . but that's just me mind-reading." Now you can see the cause of your distress—your own mind, not the situation—and can take steps to fixing things where it matters.

Consider Alternative Explanations

Don't always take your own word! Generate alternative explanations for the situation you're evaluating. Explore possibilities that aren't solely about you, and aim for realistic "best-case" scenarios. By considering different viewpoints, you can shift away from personalization or mind reading and develop a more balanced understanding of the situation. It's not that you're looking for the "right" explanation, but rather that you're getting into the habit of not assuming that your first assessment is correct, and that it is possible to think more accurately and helpfully about a situation.

To continue with the example above:

1. "My boss might be under a lot of stress because our department is busy right now."
2. "My boss might be having serious problems outside of work, and his mind isn't on his job today."
3. "My boss was being curt because he was rushing to do something else."

4. "My boss actually thought he was being friendly; he just wasn't paying much attention and greeted me carelessly. It means absolutely nothing."
5. "My boss was a little abrupt because he was just a moment ago engaging in a tricky task and is still a little flustered."

Each of your alternatives has a chance of being true, so why give more credence to one over the other, especially when you have no evidence either way?

It may well be the case that your boss *is* upset with you. But even if he was, why waste time being unhappy about it until you know for sure? The biggest lie of rumination and anxiety is that it is somehow a form of problem-solving behavior. That if we just worry about something enough, we will somehow be closer to fixing a problem or avoiding a disaster. But the truth is actually the opposite: Worrying drains your energy and makes you less efficient, less capable, less clear-thinking. Basically, it makes you a worse problem-solver. Consider that if you are concerned about what someone thinks, you can always ask them, as soon as possible, and go from there. Stewing in quiet agony about what could or might be feels like doing something, but it isn't. Only doing something is doing something.

Overcoming Generalization

The brain is an amazing tool. When working as it should, it helps you analyze situations effectively, plan and strategize, create new ideas, learn from your mistakes, organize your thoughts and feelings, and solve problems. When it's not working as it should, it *makes* problems.

Generalizing is simply the act of taking a limited piece of data and extrapolating from it so that you can make conclusions about other situations and scenarios you haven't encountered yet. So, it's what allows you to steer clear of all snakes once you've been bitten by just one. It's what lets you know that the letter "a" in one book means the same thing in another, different book. It's one of the main ways that your brain learns. It's also one of the main ways that it keeps itself trapped in its own biases, limited beliefs, and fears.

For instance, feeling humiliated after giving a wrong answer in class might lead to the belief that this will happen every time a wrong response is given. Such thought patterns can trigger overthinking and fear of humiliation in future social interactions. Here we meet another vicious cycle: You experience humiliation after speaking up, so the next time you're in class, you avoid speaking up, and the result is that you feel relief. This relief is a positive reinforcement that teaches you that avoidance and escape "works." You're more likely to keep on avoiding it.

In a way, you could look at all your fixed beliefs and ideas and trace them back to when they were just habits, or even before that, when they were just single experiences. The anxious brain is risk averse. It keeps avoiding what it thinks will bring a negative experience, all the while confirming a) that it is in fact a negative experience and b) that the only way to deal with the situation is to keep on escaping, avoiding, or using other maladaptive coping strategies.

Being free of anxious overthinking means that we don't live in our heads, but in the real, present moment just as it is. We are not constantly inhabiting an *idea* of the world and what it means—we are just here in the real world, right now, curious about how it is unfolding. We are not interpreting or reacting to our own memories of the situation, or making knee-jerk assumptions and behaving as though they're absolute truth.

We are just aware, alive, and spontaneous in the moment.

We know that each moment is entirely new, and just because things went one way in the past, it doesn't mean they are doomed to go that way forever and ever. If people can relax to actually experience the moment as it is, they may be surprised to discover that their assumptions about it were invariably far worse!

In the previous section, we saw how anxious rumination is about a narrowing of attention. In this section, we see that taking tiny amounts of data from this narrowed perception and assuming it applies to all things everywhere all the time is yet another distortion. Here are some ways to counter this tendency and let your brain go back to being something that helps rather than hinders you.

Find Counterexamples

Isn't it funny how quickly and easily we take our own word on things? Even the most naïve and trusting person will not tend to believe everything that they see or read or hear, and yet how often do we do just that when it comes to listening to our own negative self-talk?

Try to catch yourself when you're making an overgeneralization. You can recognize one in a few ways:

- It uses sweeping, absolute language like *always, never, everyone, none, forever, completely, nothing*. These words

reveal an all-or-nothing mindset that is seldom a fair reflection of reality.
- It talks in vague abstracts rather than concrete specifics. Instead of saying, for example, that you had a bad date last night, you say that you despair of the state of human connection in the modern world. This can happen so quickly you don't notice it, but pay attention and you'll see how often you're tempted to start talking about "things in general."
- It talks in terms of absolute qualities and traits instead of transitory behaviors and events. For example, you spend the morning procrastinating on a difficult task, and instead of saying "I'm having trouble with this task," you say "I'm just a lazy person. I'm an avoidant personality type. Always been that way."

When you catch yourself overgeneralizing in social situations, challenge those thoughts by actively seeking counterexamples. For instance, if you think "I always embarrass myself in front of people," recall moments when you didn't embarrass yourself and instead had positive interactions with others. If you find yourself thinking "People think I'm weird," then actively look for evidence that some people like you and some have no opinion about you at all. Sounds simple, but you'd be surprised at how unbalanced your inner dialogue really is!

Imagine a Third Party

Picture a supportive friend offering perspective on your overgeneralized thoughts. What would they say? Be the voice of reason for yourself and try to objectively assess whether your conclusions are as accurate as they feel in the moment. If you don't like that exercise, then simply imagine an even more neutral one—for example, imagine what a scientist or reporter from another planet might say about your situation. Imagine, alternatively, that you're in a court of law, and you are being questioned about "just the facts"—what would you say? Is it *really factually true* that every single person in your city is awful, or is it just that the person you went on a date with last night was?

Be Kind, Be Moderate

You may be thinking "Well, sure, but isn't it kind of true that there *is* a decline in the quality of human connection in the modern world? Aren't I a little bit right about that?"

Look for the gray area and the middle ground. Some things can be *somewhat* true, but even then we can decide how and when we focus on them. Recognize also that just because something isn't always true doesn't mean it can never be true. Instead of making sweeping statements like "I never make friends," consider more *balanced* thoughts like "I may find it challenging to make friends in some situations, but I've also had positive social interactions in the past."

You don't have to resort to phony positive thinking or be delusional (that's just more black-and-white thinking!), but simply use moderate statements. Even if your work presentation completely flopped, for example, you can say, "I didn't do well today, and that's been difficult. But I have given good presentations before, and I know I can figure out what went wrong today and do a better job next time." There is a big difference between "I have no friends" and "I haven't made friends in my new town yet."

Being realistic and honest doesn't mean we have to be unkind to ourselves! Being moderate in our thoughts is just as much about nuanced thinking as it is about self-compassion.

Stop Labeling

Your experiences come and go in your life. They are not *who you are*. They do not define you.

Today, people have more awareness and understanding of psychological concepts than ever before, but a downside of this is that many are far too quick to self-diagnose, pathologize, and label themselves in a way that only limits them and keeps them exactly where they are. Take a look at these examples to see how much of a difference it makes to talk about your *experiences* versus your *identity*:

"I'm awkward" versus "I felt nervous during that particular conversation."

"I'm a bad cook. I hate cooking" versus "I burned dinner."

"I'm an empath/highly sensitive person/introvert/Scorpio" versus "I'm feeling overwhelmed right now."

"I'm dealing with a lot of PTSD and unresolved childhood trauma" versus "Today was uncomfortable."

Can you see the difference? If you can understand your own life as a series of discrete and transitory experiences, then you never let any single episode forever determine your overall social abilities, your personality, your worth, etc. It's just something you *felt* or *thought*, not something you *are*. Thoughts, feelings, and behaviors can all change. Your permanent identity cannot.

Here is something to consider: **A more moderate way of thinking actually makes life easier**. Imagine the example above, where you have a single bad experience of feeling humiliated speaking up in class, and then overgeneralize and avoid speaking up ever again. You may tell yourself all kinds of catastrophic stories: "I always do stuff like this; it's just typical. People are never going to understand me or like me, so why bother? No one wants to help me, and I bet they're all sitting there thinking what a loser I am. I can't do it. It's hopeless. They hate me, and besides, they wouldn't get what I was saying, anyway . . ."

The brain can take a single negative experience and blow it up so large that it encompasses the entire universe and everything in it, spanning all the way into the past and persisting forever more into infinity. If you genuinely started believing yourself when you told these stories, how would you behave? If you really thought that people didn't understand you, that they were cruel and judgmental, and that you were useless and couldn't possibly improve, how would that change your behavior in life?

- You might avoid ever pushing yourself to try something new
- You'd be prone to blaming others when you failed, or just not trying at all so you never have to fail
- You'd have trouble trusting and being open with people
- You'd give up and stop making new goals for yourself
- You'd start to identify with being an underachiever, a loner, a failure
- You wouldn't stand up for yourself if mistreated because, after all, you kind of deserve it, right?
- You'd become bitter and apathetic

Taking a look at that list (and it's the kind of list that could keep growing and growing . . .), wouldn't it be easier to just live in the real world, where the discomfort only lasts a few brief minutes and then is gone forever? You could recognize that being a little embarrassed for a moment wasn't the end of the world, and then push past that transient feeling and continue to speak up, understanding that momentary discomfort doesn't imply anything about your character, your worth as a human being, or the nature of reality itself.

This may sound like an extreme example, but that is the power of overgeneralization—it can take tiny things and turn them into enormous, unmanageable ones. The next time you encounter something uncomfortable, awkward, difficult, scary, tense, or nerve-wracking, just pause and take a breath. Step back and look at your experience from the outside.

- Is the thought I'm having or the story I'm telling helpful to me?
- Do I have any evidence for the conclusions I'm making here?
- Can I replace these thoughts with something a little more moderate?

Try to see that the option to generalize is there, available to you. But you don't have to choose it.

Summary:

- Often a problem with socializing is really a problem with anxiety on a deeper level. Over-analyzing and rumination is common. If we solve the underlying anxiety problem, we free ourselves up to improve our social skills, just as we would any other skill.
- While anxiety narrows and restricts our attention and awareness, socializing requires we open our

attention and engage more fully with our external environment.
- Social rumination is a cycle; to break it, we need to understand what maintains it. Start by admitting/accepting that your thoughts may be distorted, then separate your appraisal of reality from reality itself, and distinguish discomfort from total disaster.
- Occasional anxiety is normal; it's not dangerous or the end of the world. Embrace imperfection and vulnerability, and question whether there's any evidence for negative assumptions, conclusions, and judgments. Your expectations may be unrealistic, your standards too high, or you may be ignoring/discounting the positive.
- The spotlight effect is a cognitive distortion where people overestimate how much others notice and care about their behavior in social situations. Try to expand your awareness so that you're not the center of things, and make your appraisals less *personal*, less *pervasive*, and less *permanent*.
- Discern between thoughts, feelings, and reality, and consciously consider alternative explanations—sometimes,

it's necessary to simply tolerate ambiguity and uncertainty.
- Finally, generalization is taking a limited piece of data and extrapolating from it to situations you haven't encountered yet. With distorted thinking, overgeneralization can create anxiety. Continually seek out counterexamples of any foregone conclusions you're making, be kind to yourself, be moderate, and refuse to let isolated experiences define you completely.

Chapter Two: Getting out of Your Head

Curiosity Is Medicine

Imagine for a moment a golden Labrador puppy. Picture in your mind how such a puppy moves in the world, what it does, and how it treats every new encounter. Can you envision it bouncing excitedly from one new thing to the next? Can you see how it explores, runs around, and puts its nose all over the place, sniffing *everything*?

The way a Labrador puppy explores its environment is the same way that all healthy animals explore theirs—human animals included. The natural default mode for organisms of all kinds is to engage with the environment. To seek out mates and food; to explore and uncover something new and unknown; to ask, in a way, "What's here for me?"

If this vitality, engagement, and interaction with the environment is what characterizes normal healthy animals, then it's *detachment* that characterizes unhappy, unhealthy ones. When people are depressed or anxious, they are not engaged with their environment in this way. They lose their interest in the world and in other people, and turn only inward. They lose any lust for life, any striving, and any ability to interact, even physically moving less.

Try to imagine, then, that **anxiety is a problem of misdirected attention**.

Every being comes into the world with energy and life in them, and they can direct this toward actions that help them achieve their goals. They use this energy to solve problems, to overcome adversity, to create new things, to power their learning, and ultimately, to get them what they want out of life. But sometimes, this energy gets turned inward and gets trapped there, perhaps in endless loops that go round and round and never seem to amount to anything.

For the socially anxious, the curious state of mind is like medicine. It gets you out of your head and back into the world, where you can start acting, engaging, learning, creating, communicating. In fact, some theorists say that disengagement from the world is not a symptom in depression and anxiety, but a cause—i.e., people become depressed or anxious precisely because they have forgotten how to engage with the world in healthy ways.

In the previous section, we looked at an example of post-event rumination. The truth is that such rumination is most likely to happen when the interaction was one where the person wasn't genuinely engaged. Anxious people tend to "live fifty worries behind." Basically, they lie awake at night, unable to sleep, because they are not focused on their current tiredness and how comfortable their bed is, but on how anxious they felt at a party yesterday. But the only reason they were anxious at the party yesterday is because instead of being at that party, in the moment, they were focusing on how anxious they were and all the annoying things that had happened to them earlier in the day . . .

So there are two problems:

1) Anxiety keeps you away from the real present moment.
2) It keeps you trapped elsewhere—i.e., the past, the future, or some hypothetical place that doesn't really exist.

You set up painful feedback loops. You're not engaged in the moment, so you don't connect with others or the situation at hand. This leads to post-event rumination—which, in happening, again keeps you out of the present moment. You are continually living fifty worries behind.

The way to break the cycle is to put your attention back to where it is meant to be: the present. Be your authentic self and respond naturally and spontaneously to whatever the other person shares, without overthinking it. Speak whatever comes to mind, fully immersing yourself in the conversation and making the other person the center of your focus. Treat the interaction as the most captivating and engrossing conversation you've ever had. You may even find it's worth going further than you would think appropriate—say something unconventional, unexpected, or a little risky. Don't stew over what you're going to say—just say it.

- Use "feeling talk" rather than stating dry facts.
- Give your opinion.
- When you're complimented, enjoy it and accept it. Let other people see that it gives you pleasure.

- When you don't like something or disagree, say so. Don't make it a big deal. Just state your case.
- Don't "bite your tongue."

People who are socially anxious waste all their precious energy and time scanning and monitoring themselves. Am I sitting weird? Do people find me boring? What does my face look like right now? Do they like me? Did they find that joke funny?

Instead, turn all that energy and attention onto things in the environment. What is the other person saying? Look into their eyes and try to take in the entirety of their message—the content, their emotions, the subtler points they may be expressing. Don't think about what you're going to say next, just sink and immerse in each present moment, feeling how full it can be. Take the Labrador puppy as your role model and become curious—nosy, even!—and ask lots of questions.

The secret is that curiosity and anxiety cannot exist together. Exploring your environment is *moving* toward, "approach behavior," and anxiety is *moving away*, "retreat behavior." When you are anxious and worried about what threats there are in your environment, you are not exploring that environment but protecting yourself against it.

A few more tips:

Try Wonder-Spotting

Head out one day and go "wonder-spotting." Take your camera or phone and imagine putting on a curiosity lens so that everything you look at seems new and interesting. IS there beauty, wonder, intrigue, humor out there? All these engrossing things are here, in the present—when you engage with them, you're *not* engaging with worries from the past or fears for the future.

Once you're a pro at this, try to apply the same mindset to social situations. When you walk into a room crowded with people, consciously tell yourself, "Ooh, look at all these interesting people! Talking about such fascinating stuff!" Sure, you might not believe it one hundred percent at first, but it will still help you make the shift from perceiving threat to opportunity.

There is a kind of fatalism in anxiety—a lack of creativity. This is because when we are afraid, we are usually operating with a feeling of knowing that the worst outcome is the one that will happen, and the least enjoyable interpretation is the one that is most true. But thinking this way shuts down all the possibility and wonder of the unfolding moment. In truth, anything can happen, and we don't always know how a situation will turn out. Try to move away from "I'll fail" or "They won't like me" (boring, foregone conclusions) to a more open, more wonderous feeling of "I wonder what will happen next . . .?" This reframes uncertainty and open-endedness as enjoyable and even exciting.

Practice Empathic Curiosity

People who are good with people have learned to look at other human beings as depthless sources of wonder. Really! It's not that they universally like all people, but rather they are willing to be surprised by them. They hold it as a distinct possibility that people can be kind, delightful, interesting, entertaining, inspiring. That there is a potential for good feelings even though there may not be an instant and easy connection.

Socially anxious people, however, don't give others this chance—they have concluded with certainty that other people are judgmental, difficult, alien. Without ever checking to see if their assumptions are correct, they put thoughts into the heads of strangers and then imagine those thoughts as enormously critical and harsh. They make judgments about social interactions that haven't even happened yet.

Use empathic curiosity to challenge anxiety-driven assumptions about others. Instead of jumping to negative conclusions, wonder about the thoughts and feelings of the people involved, recognizing that everyone's experiences are unique. Be willing to acknowledge that someone out there might be having a thought you haven't ever considered having yourself. Be open to the possibility that others can have interesting things to teach you, and that they might be genuinely interested in knowing more about you, too.

If you feel anxious about interacting with new people, employ empathic curiosity by wondering what might be going on in their lives and how they might be feeling. Turn away from your own internal ruminations and engage—it's this engagement that might convince you that so many of your assumptions are unfounded. If you merely stay within your own head, though, you never give yourself the opportunity to test your assumptions against reality.

Become an Emotional Detective

Combat anxiety-driven catastrophic beliefs by thinking like an emotional detective. Deliberately look for evidence that contradicts your anxious thoughts and consider alternative explanations for situations. Take that anxious self-talk voice in your head and "put in on the stand" in a court of law. Where's the evidence? Is what it's saying strictly true?

If you're anxious about a social event, challenge your beliefs by asking yourself for specific evidence that supports your fears. Look for instances where social situations have turned out positively or differently from what you expected. Most of us are familiar enough with the tenets of CBT to know that sometimes our thoughts and beliefs can be distorted or incorrect. But our emotions can be distorted too. You may notice that you *feel* as though there is a big group that you are excluded from. Setting aside this feeling, however, is this really true? Does your feeling of not belonging necessarily mean that you have been objectively rejected or even that there *is* a "big group" at all?

Practice Curiosity-Driven Self-Compassion

Use self-compassion to unlock curiosity about your fears and worries. Acknowledge your anxious feelings without judgment and explore the underlying reasons for your anxieties.

If you feel anxious about attending a social gathering, practice self-compassion by placing your hand on your heart and just tune in to how you feel. Take your "emotional temperature" and peek under the hood of your own thoughts and see what's there. You do this not so you can castigate yourself for not thinking or feeling what you "should" but rather so that you can build awareness.

Many socially anxious people falsely believe that they are very self-aware. The truth is that they are self-conscious. When you are deeply focused inward, you are actually less aware of what is going on in the world, and even though you may be hyper-focused on what is happening in your own head, it doesn't mean you have a good handle on it.

Self-compassion means a degree of acceptance. It means you notice yourself ruminating anxiously in the moment. You say to yourself, "Oh look, I'm ruminating again. That's okay. I'm just turning my attention outward again." That's all. Self-compassion means noticing when your attention has gone awry or where you have become hypnotized by your own negative self-talk, and just treating that with calm, relaxed indifference. The idea is not to beat yourself up when you notice that you are anxious; instead be glad when you become aware of your overthinking, and smile on the inside as you gently pull yourself back to the moment again. Be kind to yourself and recognize the value of that moment of awareness, rather than judge the lack of awareness that came before.

The next time you're in a potentially stressful situation, play a little game where you deliberately turn all your attention and awareness outside of yourself, away from your internal ruminations. Become the fascinated puppy and sniff around everything. Look people in the eye. See if there's anything that seems interesting or juicy or fun or intriguing, and follow it! If you do this, you might notice that later on, when the event is over, you feel much less inclined to return to it and ruminate over how it went. You don't need to "go back"—because you were *there* the first time around.

Do the Opposite

When we're anxious, we behave as any sane person would behave in the face of a threat: We retreat. We escape, avoid, or if we can't get away, hunker down and adopt a protective stance. Though this tendency is a good idea for things that are genuinely dangerous, it doesn't help us when we are facing something we only *perceive* to be dangerous.

Anxious people tend to do something to try to escape. They want to get away from the situation they believe is creating that discomfort, and eventually, they also want to escape that feeling of discomfort itself. They seek safety. And while avoiding the thing they fear may feel good in the sense that they do avoid that anxiety, what they are really doing is teaching themselves that there really is something to fear—they are reinforcing their incorrect perception.

To recover, we need to do the opposite! It follows that "facing your fears" is literally the last thing you want to do, but it must be done precisely because doing so will start to teach you that your original appraisal of the situation actually wasn't accurate.

Opposite action engages you with the world in a specific way—it gives you the chance to gather up new experiences that go against your assumptions. For example, you may have the belief "I hate socializing; it's always awkward." Unless challenged, you'll go on having this belief, and especially go on thinking that socializing is a scary, unpleasant thing, and it's always more comfortable to stay clear. But if you push yourself little by little to socialize, you start to gather up episodes where you didn't in fact hate it, and experience moments when you weren't awkward, but perfectly comfortable. Gradually, the belief starts to shift.

The key here is that it *will be uncomfortable*—by definition!

If you want to cancel on a social event and stew at home instead, don't—go out.

If the store looks crowded and you want to turn around and run home without doing your shopping, don't—head in there and get it done.

If you want to cancel your vacation rather than having to deal with the airport, don't—make a plan and get on that plane.

This is the *only* way to convince yourself that there isn't any danger. Again, it will feel uncomfortable—you may sometimes feel like kicking and screaming all the way through it—but do it anyway. It doesn't have to come easily; you don't have to like it. You might feel sorry for yourself and watch your mind come up with four million excuses and justifications for why you really, really cannot do it . . . but do it anyway. Then, when it's done, pause for a moment and ask yourself, was it that bad? Did you cope? Did you maybe even find that once you got going, it was far more manageable than you thought?

This tactic is all about recognizing that excuses are just more avoidance.

Just take a step back and notice the stories you're telling yourself. Sometimes, when anxiety is really pronounced and has been embedded in place for a long time, people can convince others very well of their excuses. For example, those with agoraphobia might shut down any suggestions that they leave the house with accusations that they are being bullied, that nobody understands them, that people are being cruel, that nobody understands how genuinely valid their reason for not going out is, and so on and so on. The point is, however, to be committed *to not fooling yourself*, even if you can fool others! You might be able to make an excuse and tell people you're sick or that you have work to do or whatever the case may be, but be honest with yourself. Can you gently challenge your excuse, not for their sake but for yours?

In CBT, we acknowledge that **thoughts, behaviors, and emotions all mutually impact one another.** Change one and you change the other two. That means that if you change your behavior, your thoughts and feelings cannot help but be affected. Sometimes, when we're anxious we sit around and wait until we feel better, assuming that our thoughts and feelings have to be just right before we can act. But it can also go the other way—by acting first, we can gradually start cultivating the kinds of thoughts and feelings we want.

This may seem counterintuitive, but it works. *When you feel anxious, behaving in an anxious way only makes you feel more anxious.* However, if you engage in opposite-to-emotion behavior, you dampen that anxiety. Let's look at a step-by-step process for opposite action.

Step 1: Ask if the thoughts and emotions are helping you
Emotions are there for a reason. They keep you safe and inspire you to values-driven action. But not all emotions are this useful—some just get in the way. Pause to discern which kind of emotion you're feeling. Is it appropriate to the situation? Is it going to bring you closer to your goals in any way? You may in fact decide that it can (for example, your anger is useful because it allows you to assert boundaries that keep you safe). But if this is honestly not the case, then opposite action might work.

Step 2: Find your urge
Emotions push you to action. What is this emotion urging you to *do*? Often, social anxiety pushes us to retreat, avoid, escape, withdraw, hide, or shut down. Notice what this urge is and define it clearly.

Step 3: Engage *completely* in the opposite of the urge
This is important—you are not trying to do the opposite of the emotion, but the opposite of the urge, which is an *action* or a concrete

choice. The urge could be canceling an outing, avoiding a difficult conversation, lying about how you feel, biting your tongue, turning down a much-wanted job promotion, or taking four days to respond to an email.

Look at the urge and do the opposite: Go on the outing, have the conversation, share how you really feel, speak up and tell the truth, accept the job, or write an immediate response to the email. And when you do it, do it completely—no half measures. It's worth pointing out that none of these actions is good or bad in themselves. For some people, going to a social event *is* their initial, escapist urge, and their opposite action would be to stay home and face what they're avoiding there.

Step 4: Give the opposite action a chance, then reappraise
Really commit to that opposite action and give it a fair try. It's okay if you're feeling terrified and want to scale things back a bit, though. For example, your urge is to cancel the party and not show up at all. The opposite action here is just to go to the party, but you can agree with yourself that you will go and stay for merely an hour, or even just half an hour if you're really intimidated. However, once you've decided, make that deal with yourself and follow through.

The point is not to punish yourself (this will only further cement this idea as negative in your mind) but to give yourself an opportunity to experience something other than anxiety. When you come back from the party, note how you feel. Is it any different from before you went? Did the event play out differently to how you imagined? Take a look at your beliefs, thoughts, and feelings about this party and see whether they still hold.

You probably won't spontaneously turn into a social butterfly overnight, but you *will* gradually chip away at the distorted beliefs and thoughts that are not really serving you. The next time you catch yourself saying, "Oh but I hate socializing. It's always awkward . . ." you might not believe it quite as much as you did before.

A Caveat
Let's say you do have an issue with going to parties and you follow the above steps exactly as they're written. You head out to this party . . . and have a bad time.

Now what?

Try to remember that the point of the exercise is not to force yourself to feel a way that you don't feel. It's about breaking down the impulse to avoid and escape—i.e., what you *do*, not what you feel. In this sense, the moment you leave your house and head to the party, the experiment has been a success—how the party turns out is secondary.

Another subtle point is that we are trying to develop a realistic, healthy attitude to the environment. And let's be honest, sometimes the outside world *is* boring, difficult, stressful, or unpleasant in some way. Sometimes we worry that we won't have much in common with people, and it turns out we don't. But that doesn't mean that engaging was wrong.

You are trying to teach yourself that social interactions, although they may be unpleasant and not what you had hoped for, are not dangerous and not a threat. In other words, they are not something we need to actively avoid in order to protect ourselves. It's a little like weather—sometimes we may get caught in the rain, but that doesn't mean we shouldn't ever go outside or that there aren't great things out there that we want to interact with.

If you find yourself experiencing a genuinely unpleasant social situation, then seize your chance: Here is an opportunity to just *sit with* your feelings without trying to escape them. Don't worry about pretending that you're enjoying it when you aren't. Don't fold in on yourself trying to guess what you did wrong, or chastise yourself for XYZ. Just notice how you feel, accept it, and move on. The trick is to see that *even if* social situations are difficult or boring sometimes, that still doesn't mean you have to escape or avoid.

Perhaps you come home and adjust your belief: "Man, I really dislike boring get-togethers like that, but you can never tell how an event is going to happen. Oh well. I still enjoy some kinds of socializing, and the next time may be more fun."

In this way, socially intelligent and well-regulated people are actually masters at dealing with disappointment and discomfort. They feel the unpleasantness, but they don't generalize it to anything else, they don't assume it means something awful about themselves or about others, and they don't treat it as a threat to be avoided in the future.

A little tip: you may find that you enjoy social situations far more when you are able to spontaneously and authentically experience and express your own true emotions. For example, if you're feeling tired, don't force yourself to act more energetic than you are. If the conversation feels dull, speak up and try to share something you're passionate about. If you're not being listened to, be a little forceful and don't allow others to interrupt you. If you engage in this way—assertively and honestly—you may find that you enjoy other people far more. You may discover that what you were trying to avoid was the effort of being inauthentic!

Challenge Your Inner Critic

By now, most of us are at least somewhat familiar with the concept of a negative "inner voice" and how what it says might not always be true or in our best interests. But while the concept is pretty easy to grasp on an intellectual level, it can take some practice to really learn to notice the voice of that inner critic and continually recognize that it needn't be a part of you—but something that you can *take a step away from and look at from the outside.*

While it's useful to recognize that you have an inner critic, progress happens when you genuinely experience real psychological distance from it. If you think, "Well, I don't really have an internal voice. I don't talk to myself," what this suggests is that you have come to "listen" to that voice to such an extent that you don't notice it as a voice at all—you mistake it for a neutral appraisal of reality.

Internal Family Systems is a therapeutic model that suggests that each person is a little like a community of smaller parts—a family. We have certain parts of us that look after certain other parts, aspects of our personality that are braver than others . . . and certain facets that criticize and judge other facets. It's a real problem when one part of you is actively bullying and abusing another part!

Your inner critic is there for a reason, however. Think of it as an internalized parental voice—one that is trying hard to keep you safe, to spare you from danger, embarrassment, and loss. In its own way, this voice is really trying to help. Because there's always the tiniest grain of truth and usefulness in what the inner critic tells us; we can go a long way in life genuinely believing that it's impossible to function without it. We might think, "How else could I ever be disciplined/brave/productive/cautious without it?"

But people who are socially anxious often engage in black-and-white, all-or-nothing thinking, and in this case it can show up as the unquestioned thought "Either I judge and criticize and hate myself, or I'm an arrogant narcissist or lazy or selfish." The real distortion is not one extreme interpretation or the other—it's the mistaken belief that there are only two possible interpretations.

So, as an example, we may want to strike up a conversation with someone we're attracted to, but the inner critic tells us, "Forget it. They're out of your league and you're going to make a fool of yourself. You're just going to be awkward and weird." Let's say that you become aware of this voice, however, and decide to challenge it. You read a popular self-help book on dating and start studying people you consider successful with the opposite sex. You decide to replace your negative self-talk with versions of the following: "I'm awesome, and they're lucky I'm even showing them attention. I don't need anybody, because I'm ultra-confident in my own self-worth. I'm invincible."

Let's say you finally strike up a conversation with the person who previously intimidated you . . . and they're not interested. Now what?

Too many people think that "challenging your inner critic" means systematically replacing every shred of fear, caution, doubt, and so on with unbridled optimism. In other words, you think "I'm a loser" and so replace it with "I'm amazing." But this is merely replacing one cognitive distortion with another.

Rather than thinking of your inner critic as a voice you constantly have to argue against, no matter what it says, think of it as something to have a conversation with. The goal is not to become relentlessly optimistic or "positive" no matter what. The goal is to adopt a frame of mind that is reasonable, rational, useful, and healthy. The better it aligns with reality, and the more able it is to respond adaptively and dynamically to that reality, the better. A big reason to adopt this attitude is simple: It has the best chance of actually sticking! Anyone who's ever tried to argue back with their inner critic with empty affirmations knows how flimsy they can appear when taken out into the real world.

In reality, there are such uncomfortable truths as the fact that sometimes people will dislike you, often for no justified or even discernible reason. Sometimes you will be rejected or disappointed. Even if you do feel confident in yourself, you will inevitably have moments of doubt, embarrassment, or confusion. A healthy frame of mind allows you to navigate these inevitable human experiences with grace and flexibility; it's not one that allows you to escape them completely or pretend they don't exist.

Navigating the Gray Area
Step 1: Become aware

Without any appraisal at all (that means criticism *or* praise), just notice what you are doing, thinking, and feeling. Notice what you are saying to yourself and accepting as true. The inner critic seldom speaks in grammatically correct, full sentences, like a little angel or devil on your shoulder.

Sometimes, it's more about images and ideas, vague feelings, assumptions, beliefs, and foregone conclusions. Just notice it with curiosity. When does it show up? Does it sound like someone you know or once knew?

Step 2: Ask questions

The aim is not to identify an "irrational thought" and immediately stamp it out with its logical opposite. Rather, imagine that this attitude, set of beliefs, or thoughts is a person—someone who might literally come to visit for dinner one day. Imagine it sitting at the table and making conversation. You could ask it two questions:

1. What are you trying to tell me?
2. What are you worried will happen if I don't listen to you?

Most likely, asking these questions will reveal that this part of you is coming from a place of **fear** and is trying to protect you. Genuinely try to look at this attempt with understanding and compassion. Immediately, you will see that the negative inner voice is not an enemy to vanquish, but more like a misunderstanding to clear up. The threat it perceives may even have some basis in reality, but the only way you can better understand this is to unpick it all with clarity, compassion, and curiosity.

Step 3: Thank your inner critic . . . then get a second opinion

In your imagination, when you notice that inner voice piping up, say to it, "Thank you, I hear you. I know you're worried for me and trying to help. Thank you for looking out for me." Then, at least according to the Internal Family Systems model, you can ask that part of you to take a step down while another part steps up and takes control. This part can be your Inner Champion—the voice that speaks up for you, challenges your blind spots gently but firmly, and helps you tackle problems maturely and systematically. Whether you envision this other voice as a sagely guru, a rational and intelligent adult, a creative problem-solver, or a supportive cheerleader is up to you.

Your original inner voice might say something like: "The people you're attracted to are out of your league. Forget it. If you talk to people, you're going to make a fool of yourself. You're just going to be awkward and weird."

You stop and think, "Aha! Is that you, Inner Critic?"

You pause and start to notice it, and eventually you can recognize its particular voice whenever it pops up—usually in social situations. You don't want to shut this voice down, but ask it with kindness and curiosity what it's actually trying to tell you. You enter into a little dialogue.

"I'm trying to stop you from speaking to them because they'll reject you, and then you'll feel bad. I don't want you to feel bad. Better you never speak to them."

"Thank you, Inner Critic. I can see you're trying to help me. You don't want me to get hurt. But I wonder if it's really true that if I speak to them, they *will* reject me."

"Of course they will! It'll be excruciating and you'll never recover."

"Hm. Sounds a lot like those cognitive distortions I've been hearing so much about. Let me check in with my inner sage and ask what they think."

"What do I think? Well, let's be real—the only way to know if someone is interested is to talk to them, right? And there's a chance they're *not* interested. But hey, why are we stressing about this? Let's just relax and talk to people. You're not proposing marriage—just strike up a conversation, ask questions, and see how it goes. Get to know them a little better."

"Yeah, when you put it like that, it doesn't seem like such a big deal. But what if they do reject me?"

"Well, they might. But what if they don't? You'll be okay either way."

In this way, your inner critic actually becomes your teacher—noticing it is an invitation to engage and adapt. By learning to dialogue with your inner critic, and letting your wiser, more rational self engage with it, you are developing emotional self-regulation. And as you can see, this is not about purely "positive" or "negative" thoughts—it's more about finetuning that ability to engage flexibly with your environment.

The biggest reason that anxiety is difficult to treat is that it's never one hundred percent wrong—the world is filled with potential threats and dangers. However, when you start from the understanding that your anxiety is actually there to help you, it's possible to selectively throw away what is distorted and unhelpful, while still retaining a healthy and balanced appraisal of risk and threat. The part of you that does this consciously is the part of you that needs strengthening. It's the part of you that grows when you get into the habit of asking the following questions:

- Is this a fact or a perception?

- What evidence do I really have for the conclusions I've just come to?
- What am I really afraid of?
- How likely is that to really happen?
- If it did happen, would it be as bad as I think it will be?
- If it did happen, is it really true I'd be unable to cope with it?
- Am I being unnecessarily hard on myself right now?
- Are there positive aspects of this situation that I have forgotten?
- Am I making assumptions? What if I stop making them?
- How would a friend or a neutral third party describe this situation?
- Is my perception colored, or am I seeing things clearly?
- Is there a more realistic, useful, and moderate way of looking at things?

Accept Yourself

When you notice your own anxiety and then rush in to condemn it, you are only adding to your own troubles. When you feel afraid, worthless, sad, or angry, you do nothing to improve the situation if you then judge yourself for feeling that way. One big way that people judge themselves is, ironically, they demand that they pretend to be happier, more positive, or more confident than they really are.

Compare this:

A: "I'm so nervous right now that I just want to crawl up into a ball and die."

B: "Don't be silly, there's nothing to be afraid of! Chin up."

To this:

A: "I'm so nervous right now that I just want to crawl up into a ball and die."

B: "That's okay. It's normal to find some situations nerve-wracking. Take a deep breath and take a small step at a time. You're doing great."

Self-acceptance is not a reward we earn by being better people—it's something we adopt because we know, on a deep level, that **we have unconditional worth as human beings, no matter what.** We are allowed to have both good and bad qualities, we recognize that we are always in the process of learning, and we are imperfect—and it's okay.

The easiest way to get a handle on this feeling of compassion is to imagine how you feel toward someone you love completely. Imagine all their flaws and weaknesses. Imagine how they have made mistakes in the past and how they occasionally feel afraid or confused. Now, ask yourself if any of this makes them less worthy or less loveable in your eyes—probably not, right? Try to look at yourself with the same tenderness and kindness.

Make a list of your good points and keep it somewhere so you can read it now and then to remind yourself of all the good you bring to the table. Remind yourself of the hardships you've already overcome, and all the things that you and only you can be. Forgive yourself. It's possible you made a mistake and did something wrong. And it's possible that you're a good person who deserves love and respect and who is learning and improving every day. Both things can be true!

Give yourself permission to be "in progress." Let go of people, situations, or old beliefs that are trapping you in unrealistic expectations. Sometimes the hardest thing is to abandon all-or-nothing, catastrophic thinking and get to work on the real, specific problems in our lives, one by one, in a sane and rational way. With self-compassion, we find a moderate, middle way that replaces extremes with more pragmatic solutions. The irony is that truly socially confident people rarely think "I'm awful" or "I'm brilliant." Rather, they're seldom thinking of *themselves* at all—because they're busy out in the world, taking action and engaging with others and life.

Summary:

- Anxiety is a problem of misdirected attention, an excessive tendency to turn inward, and a detachment from the living, dynamic environment—it's living "fifty worries behind."
- For the socially anxious, the curious state of mind is like medicine. It gets you out of your head and back into the world, where you can start acting, engaging, learning, creating, and communicating. To counter social anxiety, aim always to reconnect with the present moment.
- Practice expressing yourself more freely and spontaneously, and engage in deliberate "wonder-spotting," where you turn your curious mind out into the world and away from anxious inner rumination.
- We need to acknowledge that anxiety primes us to escape/avoid, and consciously do the opposite. Figure out how you feel and what your first impulse is, then act in the opposite way, giving yourself a chance to genuinely experience something different to see what happens.

- Progress is achieved when we learn to recognize our inner critic and gain psychological distance from it, seeing it as something you can have a fruitful conversation with. Become aware of distorted, overly critical thinking and practice curiosity without judgment: What is your inner critic trying to tell you? What is it worried will happen if you don't listen to it? Thank it for trying to help, but consciously look for healthier, more reasonable alternatives to its negative interpretation.
- Challenging distorted or critical self-talk is something you can do from a place of compassion; you can accept how you feel and look for ways to change without condemning yourself.

Chapter Three: Engage Again

Visualization

The good news: if you're an overthinker, you're already a master at visualization.

The bad news: you've been imagining only the worst possible things!

Mental visualization is an incredibly powerful but underused technique. While many overthinkers are Olympic-level catastrophizers and "what if" aficionados, they are much less adept at imagining what *could go right* and what it would look like for them to not only cope but thrive.

Your own visualization abilities can be likened to a personal VR system. **It's how you reconnect with the power of your own mind to create your experience**. Instead of being reactive and responding passively to the world as it unfolds (usually in ways we don't like or find scary), we proactively create the kind of experience we most want to have, and adjust ourselves internally to make that possible.

There are many different ways to use visualization, and for different purposes. Most techniques assume one of two primary forms:

1. Creating relaxation, emotional regulation, and a feeling of calm to cope with and counter social anxiety, whether prior, during, or after an event.
2. Imagining in vivid detail a scenario you'd like to make more real in your life.

We can visualize in order to make a difficult situation easier to manage, or to flesh out in our mind's eye a situation that doesn't yet exist, but we'd like it to. Let's consider the first type.

Creating Your Safe Space
Anxiety is not "all in your head." Thoughts and feelings may seem abstract, but the anxiety response is first and foremost a physiological reality—that is, it's *all in your body*.

The entire reason you can feel anxiety at all is because your ancestors experienced a survival advantage in possessing a system that allowed them to respond to dangerous situations. The fight-or-flight mechanism serves a vital purpose: Your sympathetic nervous system activates to prepare the body for survival action. Your digestion pauses, your blood vessels dilate, your heart rate soars, and your body fills with tension and alertness. You spring into action, defend yourself, or flee the threat. Your system calms down again, and all is well.

Except in some cases, we simply stay in that mode of hyperarousal because we *keep activating our sympathetic nervous system* with anxious thoughts. Human beings, then, have a unique ability to terrify themselves— they respond to the thought of a dangerous situation in exactly the same way as they respond to a real dangerous situation. That's why you can be at a party filled with happy, friendly people, yet your body is responding in the same way it would if it were alone in a jungle at night, surrounded by vicious animals.

Once your anxiety response has already been triggered this way, it can be very difficult to try to reason with yourself . . . that is, until you're calm again. When you're anxious, you might think, "I'm terrified because this situation is terrifying." The truth, however, is closer to: "I'm interpreting this situation as a threat *because* I'm already hyper-aroused." Remember that anxiety and tension narrow one's focus. Panic can tighten it into a mere pinprick and make it so that any stimulus at all feels dangerous, whether it is or not.

Visualization can help. It can help us downregulate that psychological anxiety and bring our entire nervous system back into a restful state again. From there, we can start to appraise our environment more rationally and neutrally.

The "safe space" visualization is about soothing hyperarousal and activating the *para*sympathetic nervous system—i.e., the "rest and digest" response. The goal is to slow your heart and respiration rate, relax the blood vessels, and release tension. This makes it easier to deal with any social situation because you are then not responding from a place of threat. You are also better able to move ahead with more adaptive coping strategies and genuinely enjoy yourself. Try this:

Step 1: Create your space

Get comfortable and relax for a moment, eyes closed. Spend some time vividly creating your own safe space in your mind. It can be anything you like as long as the place is associated with joy, peace, safety, or happiness for you. It can be a real place, somewhere made up, or a mix of both. Take your time to imagine with as much clarity as possible the sights, sounds, tastes, textures, and smells of this place. Imagine yourself immersed in this place and whatever you're doing there. Explore how you feel when you're here and what kind of thoughts you're thinking. Imagine your body is peaceful, comfortable, perfectly relaxed. Don't just watch yourself from afar in this place; literally try to see the scene through your own eyes and through your point of view.

Step 2: Make a doorway to this place

As you're imagining your special place, try to form an association or connection with a particular trigger word, image, or gesture that you can use to remind yourself of the place later. For example, you can repeat a word or mantra to yourself as you imagine the place, or make a small gesture with your fingers to act as an "anchor." An alternative is to picture a single symbol or item that represents the entire scene, like a circle or a feather. Tell yourself that this word, gesture, or symbol encapsulates all the good feelings connected to this place. Come out of your imagination and try to "test" this trigger by seeing if you can recall your safe place by thinking of the symbol or word.

For example, you can imagine in detail a beautiful, serene castle in the clouds and connect all its wonderful feelings of wellbeing with the phrase "all is well." Once the connection is made, you practice it a few more times, saying the phrase to yourself and recalling the pleasant scene and, most importantly, the thoughts and feelings that it creates for you.

Step 3: Use the trigger in a real situation

Now you can use this trigger word, symbol, or gesture as a little button that you can push any time you want to activate a mindset of calm—that is, your parasympathetic nervous system. Let's say you're starting a new job and you're intimidated by your new coworkers. On the subway ride to the office, you mentally repeat to yourself "all is well, all is well" until you start to conjure up the special place. Soon the full image comes to mind, and along with it many pleasant feelings of calm and acceptance. You carry that feeling with you into the office and find that it's much, much easier to engage with people without excessive anxiety.

The idea is that you are learning to consciously control your anxiety response, rather than being at its mercy. You set up feedback loops where you broadcast an attitude of calm and relaxation, and people respond accordingly, putting you further at ease.

Bringing Your Goal to Life

What you focus on expands. What you ignore diminishes.

Visualization is a way to use the power of your imagination to literally build new neural pathways in your brain and practice a different way of being, of thinking.

To continue our example, you could use visualization to picture yourself as you'd like to experience the first day of your new job. In the same way as you imagined the safe place, imagine your workplace in as much detail as you can, and in this picture, see yourself behaving as you want to behave. Really absorb yourself in the vision of you being confident, talking with ease, responding to questions naturally, enjoying meeting your new colleagues, and showing a lively interest in every new task and challenge.

Take this further and even imagine yourself getting the first flutters of social anxiety. But in your vision, you are in control—you rehearse how you will respond when/if this happens. You picture yourself noticing the slight anxiety, and remind yourself to breathe. You picture exactly how you cope with the situation, and watch as you move, step by step, through the problem and out the other side, in whatever way works for you. You picture yourself coming home at the end of the day, feeling tired but proud of how you mastered the situation.

Rehearsing this way—including actively rehearsing what you'll do to face difficulties or unexpected anxious feelings—gives you an enormous sense of empowerment and control. The next morning, as you embark on your first day, you find that you're responding to the situation much better—almost as if you've done it before! And when you encounter a little moment of nervousness, this, too, you recognize, and you're not thrown by it, but simply take a deep breath and respond as you planned to.

Naturally, you might want to combine both these types of visualization. Start by imagining your safe place, complete with anchor, and then move on to imagining how you'll respond in a particular situation. The great thing about visualization is that it can be what you want it to be. Whatever you're struggling with, make the commitment to yourself that you won't avoid and resist it, but instead become curious and use the "VR headset" of your own imagination to practice and rehearse the kind of response you most want to have. The more creative and curious you are, the more you can make your own brain work for you rather than against you.

How to Use Role-Playing

When we visualize, we are rehearsing certain behaviors mentally and slowly starting to make healthier alternatives real for ourselves. Role-playing takes that one small step further and asks that we begin to *act out* that alternative way of coping with a scenario.

A new study published in the *Journal of Behavior Therapy and Experimental Psychiatry* suggests that experiencing anxiety-provoking social situations from another person's perspective can be beneficial for individuals with social anxiety disorder (SAD) (Abeditehrani et. al., 2021). The authors characterized SAD as a set of negative beliefs about one's social abilities and the fear of being judged by others.

The researchers found that **people with SAD tend to exaggerate negative perceptions by others and believe the consequences of these judgments are worse than they actually are**. Addressing these negative cognitions is crucial for the effective treatment of SAD.

The study suggests a novel way to do just this: role reversal. Participants engaged in a role-playing task acted out social interactions, but switched roles with another person. By doing so, they were more able to correct their negative and distorted beliefs about being judged by others, which is a big part of social anxiety.

In the experiment, thirty-six socially anxious adults were asked to think about a social situation they might find difficult—i.e., one in which they might worry about being judged. Each participant was then asked to write a list of all the things they worried the other person might be thinking about them and how they might judge their social skills (or lack thereof). One half of this group was asked to play out this scenario with another person, while the other half was asked to play out the situation but with the roles reversed. So, the socially anxious person was asked, in the second group, to occupy the perspective of the person they had just guessed would be judgmental.

Interestingly, both groups showed an improvement in the perception and negative beliefs of the study participants—but it was the role-reversal group that most strongly felt that their original beliefs were now so much less believable than before the role-play. Simply, they just didn't think that such judgments from others were as likely to happen as they had originally thought. Putting themselves in the other person's shoes acted as a kind of challenge, disputing automatic thoughts and assumptions.

Though the article is mainly about role-play as a therapeutic tool, the technique is definitely something we can use in everyday life, whether we run through a role reversal in our own imagination or enlist the help of a friend or family member. You can try this exercise yourself the next time you're fretting over a situation that's already passed, or worrying about one that's yet to happen. Here's how:

1. Write down all the things you're worried they might think, say, or do. Just brainstorm for a few moments and put down everything in black and white.
2. Close your eyes and imagine that you're the other person (or pick just one if there are multiple other people). Think of what they're trying to achieve in the interaction, what they're focused on, what their values, worries, and goals are, and how they're likely to interpret the interaction.
3. Take a look again at your list and, still inhabiting the perspective of the other person, see how accurate the

statements are. Cross out any that you now don't feel are all that accurate.
4. You can repeat the exercise again, but with another person, if there are multiple people in the interaction.
5. When you're done, notice your anxiety levels and become curious about any distortions you uncovered. Actively think of this updated list when you find yourself ruminating over a past event or stressing about an upcoming one.

Of course, to make role-play/role reversal really work, you need to take a moment to genuinely imagine a point of view that is not your own. Try to resist the temptation to put your own beliefs into the minds of other people, but rather stay as neutral as possible. For example, if you're worried that people are going to judge you for making an awkward best man speech at a wedding, zoom out and try to occupy the mindset of the bride, the groom, or a random guest. What are these people's primary concerns and focus on the scenario? What are they trying to achieve?

Most likely you'll suddenly appreciate that the bride and groom probably feel overwhelmed and won't be paying attention to every tiny detail of your speech, considering all the other millions of things on their minds at that point;

likewise, the guests are probably focused on when dinner will be served, the music, where they parked the car, the workday they have tomorrow, how uncomfortable their shoes are, whether their gift is appropriate, or their conversations with other guests. In fact, the more you hop into the minds of other people, the more you'll realize that many of them are likely doing what you're doing: worrying about being judged!

The clever reader might think at this point, "Oh but I certainly *have* judged someone in public before. It's entirely possible that people may judge me."

The answer to this is: yes, that's true. However, consider the last time you judged someone in this way. How long did your interest in them last? Did you go home that day and think about them for hours, late into the night, judging and condemning their entire character, their very worth as human beings? Or was your interest more along the lines of "thank God it wasn't me"?

There is a connection between how much we judge others, how much we judge ourselves, and how much we fear being judged by them. People who judge others and closely monitor their behavior usually do so as an extension of their own inability to be accepting and kind to themselves—it's as though they externalize that harsh inner critic's voice and project it onto other people. Then, they can't help but imagine that everyone else is doing the same to them. But really, the things they imagine other people thinking about them are nothing more than their own thoughts about themselves. To cut a long story short, the more self-accepting you are, the more you accept others and the more able you are to believe that others do not think badly of you. If you catch yourself thinking "Other people are cruel" pause and ask yourself if this says more about you than them.

Role-Play, Rehearsal, and Make-Believe
As we've seen, **cognitive distortions, faulty beliefs, and unhelpful attitudes all grow stronger the longer we allow them to go unchallenged.** If we never put ourselves in a position where our assumptions can be tested, we never get the opportunity to correct or adjust them. Ideally we would be out in the world and conducting tests and experiments on our deepest held assumptions. **But one way to gather alternative interpretations is to do those experiments in your imagination first.**

For example, you could role-play a social situation with a few trusted friends or family members—or potentially a therapist. You play yourself and they play the role of the other people in the interaction. In this way, you get to play, pause, and reverse the situation, break it down into parts, and rehearse alternative approaches. You can also desensitize yourself to stressful sensations, eventually not feeling quite so afraid as you did to start.

Ask your helpers for feedback and suggestions. Play the situation a few times over, trying a different tactic each time. You might even like to tape or record yourself to consider later. You are doing a few things at once: practicing, desensitizing, learning, and rehearsing. What typically happens is that you role-play a situation and find it somewhat awkward or uncomfortable. You note your thoughts ("That was awful. I really messed that up."). You talk to your helpers and discover that although they noticed you were a little nervous, that didn't mean they judged you or even thought anything of it. Perhaps they didn't notice at all. Maybe you rehearse setting a boundary and feel in the moment that you are being outrageously demanding and unreasonable—until you listen to the recording a day later and discover that you sound perfectly sensible.

You might alternatively uncover some useful pointers on your behavior, but in a safe and controlled way. Your helpers might make suggestions for your word choice, body language, or eye contact—all things that you ordinarily have no insight into. For example, you may role-play a scenario with a friend who later tells you that you came across as angry and disinterested—whereas in the moment you felt vulnerable and exposed. Socially anxious people are surprised to learn that others do not find them nervous but rather detached and aloof. Rather than judging them, they may themselves feel a little judged! A role-play can be a safe way to explore all of this.

There is another way that role-play can be used, and that is to *practice and rehearse a desirable alternative.* For example, you act as if you possess certain characteristics that you are still trying to develop. Perhaps you're struggling with assertiveness, and so you role-play a scenario where you speak up for yourself with confidence, conviction, and ease. You try out a new role for yourself—maybe it takes a few attempts to nail down the role properly. Of course, the goal is not to "fake it," but you would be surprised at what you're capable of when you release yourself to your imagination (many shy introverts are brilliant actors). The goal is to fully inhabit a new perspective and truly *feel* an alternative mindset. How would you behave if you were confident? What would you say if you knew that you had as much right to be in that interaction as everyone else? What facial expression would you have if you were calm and content? How would your voice sound?

If you're not quite ready to start play-acting with friends and family, you can still achieve a lot on your own. Practice in a mirror, record yourself speaking, or rehearse answering questions or making small talk. Just remember that the *best* practice is real life—the sooner you can get out there, the better.

The Power of Random Acts of Kindness

When you're anxious about social situations and overthinking them, you tend to think a particular kind of thought, one in which you are inferior, vulnerable, or otherwise exposed to some kind of threat, while other people are in the position to judge, criticize, or mock you. **Fear makes us frame social interactions in a way that assumes and predicts hostility—** we imagine that there is a glaring spotlight shining right on us, and that everyone will soon assemble to make their judgments, and we will be found deficient in some way.

There is one foolproof way to turn this attitude on its head, however: Be kind and charitable to others.

When we approach people with this mindset, we not only immediately shift our focus from our own anxious, introspective ruminations and outward to them, we also set up an expectation that they'll respond positively to us. This collapses the "me versus them" framework and takes the pressure off you, placing emphasis instead on your *actions*, which are deliberately chosen to foster a feeling of trust and friendliness. It works not just because it's a good idea to be kind (which it obviously is!) but because it forces us out of our heads and into *positive* anticipation of what the interaction can be.

Instead of ruminating over thoughts like "What will they think of me?" we *think of them*—and we ask instead, for example, "I hope they like the gift. What else do they need? I want them to feel good."

Canadian researchers Jennifer Trew and Lynn Alden conducted a study published in Springer's journal *Motivation and Emotion* that suggests that engaging in acts of kindness can benefit individuals suffering from social anxiety. Social anxiety goes beyond shyness and can lead sufferers to actively avoid socializing, resulting in fewer friends, feelings of insecurity in social interactions, and a lack of emotional intimacy, even in close relationships.

The study focused on whether performing acts of kindness could reduce anxiety levels and facilitate easier engagement with others over time. Undergraduate students with high levels of social anxiety were randomly assigned to three groups for a four-week intervention period. One group engaged in acts of kindness, such as helping roommates or neighbors or donating to charity. The second group had social interactions without engaging in kind deeds, and the third group had no specific intervention and only recorded daily experiences.

The results showed that the group that actively performed acts of kindness experienced a greater overall reduction in their desire to avoid social situations, especially in the initial phase of the intervention. This suggests that acts of kindness serve as an effective strategy for reducing avoidance and countering feelings of possible rejection, anxiety, and distress faster than mere exposure to social interactions.

Trew and Alden believe that interventions involving acts of kindness can help socially anxious individuals lead more satisfying and engaging lives over time, leading to changes in their disposition. By promoting positive interactions and perceptions of the world, acts of kindness contribute to increased happiness and support, which are crucial for overcoming social anxiety and building meaningful relationships.

If you're an overthinker and you're socially anxious, ask yourself, when was the last time you did something kind for someone without expecting anything in return? A random act of kindness needs to be done with absolutely zero expectation of a reward or reciprocal kindness. And the positive feelings of gratitude and warmth it generates are usually much, much stronger than feelings of self-doubt, low self-esteem, or anxiety.

This change in perspective can be a real paradigm shift for overthinkers—it reminds us that **we don't necessarily have to be ultra entertaining, charming, intelligent, or confident to make people feel good or to make a difference in their lives.** That we don't have to *perform* at all—that social interactions can be low-stakes, enjoyable, easy, and life-affirming. Too often, socially anxious people feel ineligible to engage with others socially because they see social situations as a kind of arena where they need to demonstrate a set of skills. They imagine there are many complicated and difficult rules to follow, and if they fail to follow those rules properly, they will be found out and excluded.

But have you ever noticed how children make friends with one another? Especially if they have not yet learned all those social rules of engagement, or even to speak, they still manage to quickly establish rapport with one another. Rather than thinking "Do they find me interesting? What do they think of me? Am I saying the right things? Can they tell I'm anxious?" a healthy and happy child simply thinks "What do I find interesting? What do I think of this environment? Who is this person, and how can I communicate with them?" A child may approach another child and simply give them something—there is no need for a clever pickup line or a formal greeting!

Generosity, kindness, and compassion are powerful things, and they can quickly cut through self-doubt and nervousness. **When you are focused on giving and receiving, on gratitude and empathy, your mind is *not* focused on threat.** You see much less of a barrier between you and the other person, and on the other side of that barrier isn't someone completely alien and different to you, but a fellow human being who responds to kindness and care just like you do. It starts to occur to you that people are not merely a potential source of anxiety—they can be a source of connection, pleasure, gratitude, and happiness.

If you've struggled with socializing for a long time, you can start to think of other people—of society in general—as a difficult, hostile thing that you are constantly wrestling with. But there is something beautiful about remembering why human beings communicate at all. All people want to be seen, heard, accepted, and included for the unique contributions they bring to the world. Anxious people can focus a little too much on how well they meet some arbitrary social standards, while never quite considering that they have the power to offer these things to others—we can listen to others, we can validate them, we can compliment them, and we can make them feel valued and included.

At the very bottom of every conversation and every human interaction is a need for people to be acknowledged and validated. There is a need for rapport, understanding, and respect. Start there, and everything else will fall more quickly into place. Here are a few ideas:

- Pay attention to people in your environment and notice who is struggling. Step in and quietly solve a problem for them or offer a kind gesture. If your colleague left their lunch at home, pick up a little something for them when you're out

getting food for yourself. If someone in the supermarket drops something on the floor, pick it up quickly, hand it to them, and smile.
- Spontaneously thank and praise people. Be sincere and genuine and choose something you know they value and have worked hard on, even if it's just something small. "Thanks for getting these booklets properly bound, Brad. They look really professional, and the delegates are going to find them so easy to read. Thank you."
- Pay for a stranger's coffee or groceries just because.
- Hold the door open for someone or offer someone your seat on a bus or train.
- Volunteering is great, but instead of going through a big organization, try to look around your world and see where your help is most needed. Maybe the old lady across the hall would appreciate your help once a month collecting her prescription.
- Go through your phone contacts and pick out five people you haven't spoken to in a while. Drop them a line and say something nice.
- Tidy up your home and collect a few items to donate.

- Leave a few quarters in the laundromat machines for the next person—it'll make their day.
- When you're out and about, make brief eye contact with passersby and smile warmly. Do this five times and you'll be amazed at how much it changes your mood.
- Instead of worrying if you're being awkward at a party, deliberately find the most uncomfortable-looking person in the room and make a beeline for them. Make them the focus of your attention for five or ten minutes and see how you feel.
- Actively try to connect people in your social network. Introduce people you know to one another and put in a good word for others if you know they're looking for work or starting a business.
- Express genuine gratitude to someone you might have otherwise ignored or taken for granted, like a nurse, waitress, garbage collector, or cashier.
- If you have valuable insight or know something truly useful, share it freely. Offer to help someone with a bit of technology they don't understand, do a free seminar at work, or graciously take the time to help out some lost tourists

and suggest a few places they could visit.

You're not trying to earn points, show off, or set up some kind of transaction. Rather, you're consciously choosing to create a moment founded on gratitude and shared humanity. You can take the first step and consciously choose to set that tone. **If you challenge yourself to do just one small act of kindness a day, after a month you will notice how much less threatening other people seem, and how much easier it feels to approach them**. Even grumpy-looking people will break out into a warm smile with the smallest act of kindness!

Summary:

- Visualization is a great way to reconnect with the power of your own mind to create your experience. You can cultivate relaxation and emotional regulation to better cope with and counter social anxiety before, during, or after an event, or you can use your imagination to mentally rehearse in vivid detail a scenario you'd like to make more real in your life.
- A "safe space" visualization can be a way to counter a hyper-aroused autonomic nervous system so that

you're able to think more clearly and calmly about a situation. Carefully imagine the place, create doorways and triggers into that memory, and then practice entering into the safe space at will. Visualization also helps you build new neural pathways in your brain and practice alternative ways of thinking, feeling, and behaving before you try it out in the real world.

- Role-playing takes visualization one step further, as we *act out* alternative ways of coping or engaging with a scenario. People with social anxiety tend to exaggerate other people's negative perceptions of them, but when they role-play being those other people, these perceptions tend to be corrected, and they feel less anxious.
- Cognitive distortions, faulty beliefs, and unhelpful attitudes all grow stronger the longer we allow them to go unchallenged. In role-play, we can artificially expose ourselves to counterevidence so these distortions can be weakened. You can also visualize or rehearse a desired outcome, such as making believe you possess certain social skills and practicing/exploring what that would feel like.

- Finally, random acts of kindness can reduce anxiety because they challenge the fearful way we may be approaching social interactions, and create an expectation of kindness and gratitude rather than hostility. We collapse the "me versus them" framework, get out of our own heads, and focus on positive action. This state of mind is incompatible with fear and perception of threat.

Chapter Four: Take ACTION!

Being sociable, confident, calm, and capable is not something you **feel**, it's something you **do**.

In previous chapters, we've taken a look at what anxious overthinking is, how to get out of your head and back into the world, and how to use visualization and things like role-play to bridge the sometimes scary gap between the two.

Practice and strategy are so important, but at some point, socializing is not an academic or abstract activity, but something you do collaboratively with other people. **We ultimately learn to be better at socializing by socializing—not by thinking, planning, imagining, or hoping.** No amount of insight into your childhood or sophisticated psychological theory will bring you half as close to improvement as taking the leap out into the world with others.

Put a Fence Around Your Rumination

One thing that can keep us away from taking conscious, intelligent action in this way is, obviously, overthinking it. We first ruminate about how embarrassed we were or might be, about what others are thinking of us, and whether we said something wrong or awkward. The irony is that as we become more social and take those brave steps out of our comfort zone, our rumination may *actually increase*. We may feel more strongly than ever that there is something fundamentally wrong or different about us, or perhaps that it's too late to learn, that changing is too costly, too embarrassing, or too difficult. We might find the content of our overthinking starts to shift toward making ever more convincing excuses for why we can't, we shouldn't, we mustn't.

One thing to keep in mind is that **you cannot think your way out of overthinking, and you cannot worry your way out of anxiety**. If you're doing that, all that's happening is more of the same. Rumination is like the "tar baby" in the old-school fairy tale—the more you try to wrestle with it, the more you find yourself stuck to it and unable to escape. In other words, the best way to engage with overthinking is . . . not to engage with it. Engage, instead, with the world around you.

Remember that anxiety is an ancient evolutionary adaptation that exists entirely for your survival—alarm and hyperarousal evolved precisely so that it can be *channeled into action* that will save your life. In modern terms, concerns and worries are meant to focus your mind on potential problems so that you can take steps to fix them. Unless you are converting that stress into action that benefits your life, though, your temporary fears and worries will never dissipate after serving their purpose, and will instead linger, damaging you in both body and mind. **We can understand chronic worry and rumination, then, not as an excess of thinking, but a deficit of meaningful action.**

Many highly intelligent people become trapped in patterns of rumination and overthinking precisely because they think that thinking about a problem is the same as solving it, but that is **the first lie of rumination, that worry is a kind of problem-solving behavior.** They may spend years in therapy unpicking the complexities of their childhoods and read all the right books and come up with several dozen smart-sounding reasons and excuses and justifications for why they are just "introverted" or "highly sensitive" or any of the many labels on offer today in the modern self-help market. In all this, not only do they fail to see the one thing that would improve their situation (action), they continue to reinforce all the attitudes and beliefs that will only make it harder to take action in the future. It may sound harsh, but far too many of the things we offer anxious people as solutions for overthinking are really just . . . more overthinking.

We cannot vanquish our rumination forever. The human mind was built to be alert to and focused on potential dangers and threats. That's just what it does when left to its own devices. We are all imperfect, and we are all built to desire social acceptance in the group, among other things. This is not evidence of a character flaw, and it's not some major existential threat, either. Rather, worry and anxiety are normal sometimes—it's just a question of how far you will allow it to dominate and determine your actions. Here are a few ways to put a "fence" around your rumination:

Accept It

When you judge and condemn your own tendency to stew over things, overthink, or ruminate, you just add *another thought* to the pile. Don't create more problems for yourself by stressing about stress or judging yourself for being self-critical. The moment you notice you're doing so, short-circuit that vicious cycle by taking a step back and laughing at yourself. Create that psychological distance and, with as much compassion as you can, refuse to take yourself seriously. Give your worry a name and an identity, if you like. "Oh, hello, Mildred, it's you again . . . I suppose you've come to tell me all the ways that I'm the worst person in the world again, right?"

Rumination, worry, and anxiety are human. See it and let it go. It's like the crest of a wave, in that it comes on, it intensifies for a while, and then it dissipates. Why hold on to it and make it last longer than it needs to? Acceptance allows it to pass; resistance and judgment draw it out.

Be Mindful
Overthinking is like having a mind like an untrained puppy leaping and bounding excitedly after every single thing that crosses its path, with zero discipline or self-awareness. With meditation, you can train yourself to see that **you don't necessarily have to get on board with every passing thought that comes your way. Just because you have a thought doesn't mean you have**

to keep having it. Just because a thought came along doesn't mean . . . well, anything. You don't even have to appraise whether a thought is a good or bad thought. If you want to sit peacefully and quietly, you can do that, without entertaining *any* thought.

Imagine your stream of consciousness is a literal stream. Every time you have a thought, see it as a thought and imagine it in the stream quickly washing away again, gone forever. If your thoughts start becoming a bit meta (you worry about how well you're doing, for example), just watch as *that* thought also goes flowing into the stream and away. Practice such an exercise for ten minutes a day and you will strengthen your ability to see that thoughts can and always will "pop into" our minds, but we always get to choose what happens next.

Schedule-Fixed "Worry Time"
Remember that the lie of rumination is that worry and anxiety are somehow useful, and that going over and over things in your head will somehow help you avoid disaster. It's not true. One way to remind yourself of this is to acknowledge that your worry can serve a small purpose—but that it will do so on your terms and on a schedule of your choosing.

Try this next time your mind seems to be running away with you. Imagine saying to your anxious mind, "Thank you. That's a good point. I'll make a note of it." Then take a notebook and write down a line or two to capture this worry. For example, "My in-laws are going to hate the Christmas presents I've bought them and judge me." Now, look at the worry that you've set down in the notebook and consciously tell yourself, "I don't have to worry about this anymore because I've noted it down and won't forget about it." When you catch the thought popping up in your mind later on, quickly tell it, "Oh, thanks for the reminder, but I've already sorted that out—it's in the notebook."

Then, once a day, engage in your designated "worry time." Give yourself a full, uninterrupted fifteen- or twenty-minute block of time where you do *nothing but worry* about the things in your book. The agreement is that you can do as much worrying as you like during this period, but that you won't worry outside of it, except to note things in your book for later. A few things may happen:

- You realize how utterly boring and repetitive your mind can be! At the time, it felt like a million different worries—but it's really just the same

two or three churning round and round.
- You notice how worrying about something and not worrying about it pretty much amounts to the same thing at the end of the day. So why worry about it?
- You see how some things that seemed life-or-death important in the morning suddenly seem irrelevant in the afternoon. Nothing can prove to you just how fickle and empty rumination is as seeing yourself follow it here, there, and everywhere... isn't it exhausting?
- You may begin to see that worry actually doesn't solve any problems. Either what you were anxious about never came to pass, or it was abstract and irrelevant in the first place, or it resolved itself without your anxious interference.
- You may discover that you arrive at your worry time feeling like you don't *want* to worry. Take a closer look at that feeling and ask where it comes from.

Be curious about what thoughts you keep putting down—could these be core beliefs from your inner critic that you can slowly start to challenge and reframe?

Externalize

Remember that anxiety is there to be discharged into the environment and channeled into intelligent action. When you catch yourself overthinking, ask yourself "What action will help me clear and release this anxiety?"

If you've been up all night worrying about a medical condition, stop and make an appointment with a doctor then and there.

If you're in anguish wondering what your crush thinks about you, stop and just ask them.

If you're putting off a work assignment and can't stop ruminating about how awful it will be when you miss the deadline and get fired, stop and take the first small step to starting the project. If you start ruminating again, stop and carefully think about the next step, no matter how small.

You get the idea. One outcome is that you will see that it's better to act than to worry about a million vague possibilities and potentials. Occasionally the right action is very obvious and easy to do; other times you may need to spend some time strategizing—some parts of a situation will be under your control, while other parts won't. Instead of ruminating, think carefully about your zone of control and make a plan for what you'll do next, even if you can't act right now.

A second outcome is that you'll see that you cannot in fact take action because the thing you're worried about is actually not in your control. In this case, pause and really absorb that this is the reality. You cannot do anything about the problem. If you worry about it, it is what it is. If you don't worry about it, it is what it is. Shine a clear light on the fact that continuing to worry at that point is a choice you'll be making—a choice to deliberately feel bad for no good reason.

Sometimes, externalizing takes the form of putting up a long-overdue boundary, or of choosing to let something unhealthy go from your life. Sometimes, what's needed is a conversation. When we talk to ourselves in our own heads, the conversation tends to be small, repetitive, and circular. When we talk to others, our worries can move and breathe as other people weigh in, challenge, support, or suggest something we hadn't thought of. Having a genuine dialogue is sometimes the best cure for a toxic inner monologue.

Finally, don't underestimate the power of distraction. The action you take might actually have no relationship to the ruminations. For example, many people find that once they start getting anxious and too inward-focused, they need to get outdoors and do a long run or deep clean the house or even head to the mall where they can completely forget themselves for a moment. Abruptly switch tasks and literally move to another room or out of the house entirely.

Mine Your Anxiety for Meaning
Of course, sometimes the "action" hidden in our anxiety really is a little more abstract. In this case, after ruminating on negative social experiences, try to extract any valuable lessons. Ask yourself questions like "What can I learn from this?" and "What is the lesson here?" This shift in perspective can help you move forward constructively.

Learning a lesson about an unpleasant experience is one way to get a kind of closure on it, and a way to tell your mind, "Okay, we can move past this now." Experts have theorized that those who experience PTSD revisit and reimagine the traumatizing experience because something in them wants to fix the problem, to figure out why things went wrong, and to regain some kind of control over it, even if only in hindsight. That's why so many PTSD sufferers find some relief in making meaning from their experience, whether that's going on to help and support others who've endured the same thing, activism, finding spiritual or philosophical significance in their story, rediscovering their values and principles, or enjoying the fact of their own growth and development as human beings.

On a smaller scale, you can do the same thing. Instead of, for example, stewing over the thought "I embarrassed myself like an idiot," think instead "What do I now know about how to do a presentation next time round? What can I improve on?" Shifting into a positive learning mindset makes your pain or discomfort *mean* something—and that makes it easier to move on from.

Exposure Therapy

Exposure therapy is a classic cognitive behavioral approach and is essentially an attempt to break down negative associations and conditioned responses and set up conditions where new ones can be formed. Anxiety, the theory says, is a learned and conditioned response, and that means it can be unlearned. If you continue to experience what you believe is an intolerable and threatening situation, but remain with it long enough to repeatedly see that it does not bring about the feared outcome, you gradually teach yourself that the belief "this is a scary thing" is no longer founded.

In exposure therapy, you choose to face your feared situation, and in so doing you dampen the ordinary anxiety response until it fades altogether. Sometimes, you can speed up this process by deliberately connecting the situation and the triggers in it to something positive, i.e., something other than fear and avoidance. For example, a common technique is to learn to interpret certain sensations (increased heartbeat, sweaty palms) as excitement rather than fear.

The trouble with phobias, anxieties, and all other forms of fearful avoidance is that usually the person has had plenty of opportunity to teach themselves that escaping is an effective strategy. They tend to flee feared situations, avoid them altogether, or deliberately interpret neutral stimuli as threatening. The result is that even though they may be *exposed* to the situation, they are still not learning to tolerate it. Therefore, the name "exposure therapy" is a bit misleading—it is not always exposure alone that will cure anxiety or phobia. Rather, it's the deliberate efforts we make to learn new behaviors, attitudes, thoughts, and feelings about how we respond to that exposure and how we deal with our discomfort.

Ideally, exposure therapy, systematic desensitization, "flooding," and other techniques are best practiced with a trained therapist who can ensure you're taking an approach that best fits your unique situation. But there are many tricks you can do yourself without the help of a professional, as long as you understand the basic principles.

One such trick is to use *graded* exposures, or more simply, "baby steps." Throwing yourself into the deep end and facing your worst nightmare with no warmup or preparation may backfire—because it cements in your mind the idea that the situation is indeed terrifying. If you then escape that terrifying situation without ever learning to cope with it differently, you have only reinforced your conditioned response (to escape), making it more likely next time. On the other hand, going too slowly risks leaving the old associations completely intact and confirming in your mind that they cannot be changed.

Graded Exposure: Step by Step

Step 1: Identify your fear

What is the situation, place, or activity that you are most anxious about? If there are more than one, or your fears are a little vague and diffuse, try to identify the most frightening, or pick a single concrete situation where you feel your anxiety would be highest. Work with one at a time. For example, you might decide that going to a party where you know nobody there and having to talk to strangers is the biggest issue for you currently.

Step 2: Break it down

Take this situation and break it down into different parts or variations. In our example, you might identify the following:

Going to a party where you know everyone.

Going to a party where you know just one or two people.

Going to a party where you know nobody at all.

Going to a small gathering at a coffee shop.

Going to a small gathering at a pub or bar.

Going to a smaller meeting at a good friend's house.

Going to a bigger meetup at a friend's house.

Having a one-on-one chat with a close friend at home.

Having a one-on-one chat with an acquaintance at home.

Having a one-on-one chat with a stranger at home.

Having a one-on-one chat with a stranger at a party where you know nobody.

. . . and so on.

Take your time doing this—no two lists will be the same. You want a nice mix of at least ten but preferably more.

Step 3: Rank them

Now look at the list and rank how anxious you would feel doing each of these activities, from 0 to 100, where 100 represents the most anxious you could possibly feel. Arrange the list in order, for example:

Having a one-on-one chat with a stranger at a party where you know nobody—100

Going to a party where you know nobody at all—90

Going to a party where you know just one or two people—85

Going to a party where you know everyone—83

Going to a small gathering at a pub or bar—80

Going to a small gathering at a coffee shop—72

Going to a bigger meetup at a friend's house—45

Going to a smaller meeting at a good friend's house—43

Having a one-on-one chat with a stranger at home—40

Having a one-on-one chat with an acquaintance at home—35

Having a one-on-one chat with a close friend at home—25

This exercise should help you get a clearer idea of what elements are actually having the greatest impact in a situation (in our example, big noisy party venues are more anxiety-provoking than strangers). You may not get so nuanced and fine-grained an understanding of your fear if you always escape it, however.

As you piece it together, imagine that you are building a nice, even ladder that takes you smoothly from where you are to where you want to be. A good ladder has enough steps, and the steps are roughly the same distance from one another. In our example, it might be worth brainstorming a few additional activities between a big meetup at a friend's house (45) and a small gathering at a coffee shop (72) so that the jump from one to the other isn't too overwhelming. Perhaps you decide to include a few trips to a location that you find slightly scarier than a coffee shop, but not as scary as a pub or bar. You might add "eating at a trendy restaurant during the day" and "eating at a trendy restaurant during a weekend evening when they're really busy" to the list, and rank them accordingly.

Two things to remember: the list is yours alone and will be completely subjective. Plus it's not permanent. You can make changes as you go. You might find that you need smaller/finer gradations once you start, or that a few activities can be lumped together once you discover they're not scary after all.

Step 4 (optional): Practice relaxation

Drill and rehearse any favorite technique for calming yourself down. One method is the "safe place" we've already discussed, but you can use any combination of breathing exercise, visualization, mindfulness, or muscle release to actively bring yourself to a calmer state. Whatever it is, make sure you've practiced it enough times in preparation so that you know how to access it at will.

Step 4: Begin

Start at the bottom of the ladder and do the first activity. Remember that you are not trapped or forcing yourself to do it—you are choosing to. That said, the point is to remain with the situation and *not* escape. Complete the task, and as you do so, choose to mentally coach yourself with positive, supportive self-talk:

"You're doing great."

"You're okay and you can manage this."

"You're in control."

"You're safe."

You could combine this step with other techniques already discovered, such as rehearsing ahead of time how you imagine you'll tackle this task, but also playing the role of someone who isn't afraid of the situation, and doing what they would do. As you complete the task, it's extremely important to try to dampen your anxiety response—for example, by using the relaxation technique from step 3. You might have a one-on-one chat with a friend in your home and consciously pair this with a breathing exercise and a visualization technique before and after to ground you. What you are doing is deliberately pairing the feared situation with feelings of calm and relaxation.

It *is* possible to simply stay with the situation until you no longer feel anxious, but this may take a while, and besides, you can speed up the process by proactively bringing yourself into that calmer frame of mind. Whatever you do, don't try to avoid, escape, or distract yourself. Stay with it.

Step 5: Climb the ladder

When you've completed one rung of the ladder, pause and take a moment to congratulate yourself and celebrate the milestone. You want to really feel comfortable at that level before moving on to the next one, so don't worry if you want to repeat the task a few times until you no longer feel that dread or panic. You want the task to feel neutral and easy—like you're indifferent to it.

Give yourself a little time to adapt your own self-concept and your core beliefs as you go. Especially at the higher levels, you might start to see that you are regularly encountering evidence against your beliefs and assumptions. Take the time to notice this has happened, and consciously update old beliefs to reflect your progress. Repeat these to yourself as you climb the ladder. You are giving yourself new learning opportunities, and each one is an experience that teaches you that you *can* do things you once thought were too frightening.

Stepping Outside Your Comfort Zone

Graded exposure is great for helping you overcome fears and phobias, but even if you don't have some major hangup to beat, there is a way to consciously choose to live *just outside your comfort zone*. The idea is not to continually scare the daylights out of yourself by constantly attempting really terrifying things, but to stay clear of that really boring, safe, and predictable realm. The sweet spot is somewhere in the middle—where you are gently challenged, excited, inspired, and ever-so-slightly on your toes. For example, if you're used to saying hi to a colleague and that feels easy, push yourself to say hi and just a few things more, or make a little joke. If you're used to walking everywhere with your head down, just lift your gaze now and then to make eye contact or smile at people. Instead of eating lunch alone, sit with others you ordinarily would have avoided.

What you want to do is train a general appreciation for novelty and slight discomfort, rather than teaching yourself to overvalue avoidance. You want to make *moving toward* a way of life, and continually counter a tendency to *move away from*.

- **Identify the specific behavior you want to change.** Focus on one behavior at a time to make the process manageable. Examples include texting instead of calling, avoiding eye contact, not suggesting social outings, waiting for others to initiate contact, rehearsing social interactions, or not participating in discussions at work or in class.
- **Understand why you want to change the behavior.** Recognize that discomfort may arise during the process of acquiring a new skill or learning. Stay connected to the reason behind your decision to change, which could be, for example, feeling more connected to colleagues at work.

- **Determine how you will make the change, and practice comfort zone challenges.** Decide whether you will take a big step or start with smaller, more gradual changes. Below are comfort zone challenges you can try:
    - Order food and have a quick conversation with the cashier
    - Attend a Meetup group
    - Facetime someone you haven't talked to in a while and catch up with them about their life
    - Approach a random girl/guy on the street and give them a compliment
    - Tell someone important in your life how much you care about them

Letting Go of Safety-Seeking Behaviors

From the perspective of anxiety, the solution to encountering something scary is to remove yourself from it in any way possible—run away, avoid it, or escape. This is probably a brilliant strategy when faced with a snarling wild animal who wants to eat you, but things get complicated when the thing you've decided is scary is simply other people, sharing your opinion, or being in a crowded place. In the context of social anxiety, the concept of "safety behaviors" refers to certain coping mechanisms or avoidance strategies that individuals may adopt to protect themselves from *perceived* threats or negative judgments. The emphasis here is on the perceived nature of that threat.

Usually, safety seeking and escape/avoidance behaviors get cemented as habits because, in their way, they work. For example, we may feel anxious when we're speaking up in a group of people. The situation might instantly trigger feelings of panic and discomfort, and all at once our head fills with ideas like "they're judging me" and "you're making a fool of yourself and everyone can see." So immediately you do whatever it takes to ease these awful feelings—you decide to never,

ever speak up in a group. You keep quiet, and your anxiety lowers.

The next time you're in a group, your brain sees two paths in front of it: One is to speak up and feel anxious about it; the other is to say nothing and feel safe and comfortable. Easy to see which one you'd go for, right? In fact, part of your "solution" might be to carefully convince yourself that it really is in your best interests to never share your opinion, to never contribute to group conversations, and to bite your tongue. You may start to believe that never speaking up is a more or less fixed part of your identity and can't be changed, anyway. Because avoidance and escape make you feel better in the moment, you mistake them for genuine solutions. And very quickly, you lose sight of the fact that the thing you're escaping and avoiding was never a genuine threat in the first place—the problem was your perception of the threat. The solution was to correct this perception, not to escape the "threat."

In the case of social anxiety, safety behaviors may include:

- Positioning yourself so as to avoid excessive scrutiny (e.g., hiding in the back row of the classroom or wearing dull and unassuming clothes so as not to draw attention to yourself).

- Taking on roles in social situations so you don't have to interact fully with others (for example, keeping busy and bustling behind the scenes, "helping" in the kitchen, being the one in charge of drinks so that you can constantly have an excuse to stand up and leave the room).
- Misusing alcohol, drugs, or other substances to manage anxiety.
- Endlessly checking on screens and gadgets to distract yourself and create a kind of "buffer" between you and others (a common example is to set up social interactions in front of the TV, which will help cover up awkward silences and cut down on the need for eye contact).
- Over-preparing what you want to say and rehearsing scripts (in an attempt to avoid uncertainty and spontaneity).
- Continually keeping focus on other people by asking them questions and talking about them, but rapidly deflecting when they ask about you.
- Being extremely accommodating and polite, trying to say all the right things, people-pleasing, and overly formalized or rule-bound interactions (this is an attempt to escape making a fool of yourself, being judged by others, or

inadvertently hurting or offending someone).

But safety-seeking behaviors can be even more subtle than this. Consider the following extreme example where someone is deathly afraid of doorknobs. They cannot even bear *thinking* about the existence of doorknobs, let alone seeing or touching one. When the thought of a doorknob pops into their head, they freak out and immediately start practicing a breathing exercise they learned in their meditation class to calm them down. They slow their breathing, squeeze their eyes shut, and repeat the mantra over and over: "You're okay, you're okay." Soon, they're not thinking about the doorknob anymore, and the next day when someone asks about it, they confidently say that they are working on their anxiety and making progress with their doorknob phobia.

But are they? When they act as though doorknobs are a genuine threat—one requiring immediate intervention with a complicated breathing technique—they are just confirming for themselves the fact that doorknobs really are dangerous! Avoiding a fear is not solving the problem. It may *feel* like it because you instantly relieve your anxiety, but the problem (your incorrect appraisal of threat) is just as strong as ever, if not more so.

To truly make progress with a doorknob phobia, your goal would not be to find a way to live without ever seeing one, but rather to teach yourself to progressively be around doorknobs *without allowing yourself to escape*. Only with repeated exposure to the so-called threat can you start to give yourself an experience where the worst doesn't happen. You learn to tolerate what was once feared to be intolerable. The big insight with safety-seeking behaviors is that they were never about "safety" at all—just avoidance.

Imagine a man who walks around town with a little mouse in his pocket. People ask him why, and he explains that he is terrified of elephants, and he's heard that elephants are afraid of mice. So as long as he has one, he reasons, he'll be safe. You tell him that he's being silly, because the likelihood of an elephant bothering him is extremely low. He replies that of course that's the case—thanks to his mouse! Think about what you would tell this man to try to convince him that his safety-seeking behavior (his mouse) was unnecessary. How could you convince him that the thing he was afraid of in the first place was not really based in reality? Chances are you'd say something like, "Well, leave the mouse at home for a week and walk around town, and you'll see that no elephants will bother you."

Essentially, letting go of our safety-seeking behaviors is a little like leaving the mouse at home—even though we're convinced it's the thing keeping us safe and even though we really believe that an elephant could be prowling the streets and could attack us at any moment. One more distinction before we move on: Not everyone who has a mouse is participating in safety-seeking! You need to look at your own unique situation and be clear about how certain behaviors are *functioning* in your life. One person may carry a mouse simply because they like mice and they're a little eccentric. Similarly, wearing drab clothing, drinking too much, or asking a lot of questions doesn't necessarily have anything to do with anxiety—it's about *why* those behaviors are there. You'll know a behavior is a problem if you feel disproportionately panicked at the thought of not being able to do it—that's a clue to the role it plays in your life.

Safety-seeking encompasses any behavior designed to prevent us from directly confronting our fears. They needn't be rational (they often aren't), and they needn't be pure "behaviors," either, and can include more mental avoidance strategies like denial or making excuses and justifications. Relying on these safety behaviors prevents us from ever testing the validity of our fears against reality—which can then just deepen our fears and make them more stubborn. By directly facing our fear and approaching rather than avoiding it, we have a chance to challenge our distorted predictions. Gradually, these fears lose their emotional grip and no longer dictate our actions.

Another consequence of safety behaviors is their potential to become self-fulfilling prophecies. For example, when you stay silent in work meetings to avoid making mistakes, naturally you don't make any mistakes. But that means that you never learn the lessons you might have learned from making those mistakes. You never learn to be a more confident and comfortable speaker, and you slowly lose the ability to articulate yourself properly. If you finally do speak up, you're a little rusty and more likely to stumble on your words or express yourself poorly, just because you're out of practice. You may be so good at never sharing your opinion that when you finally do, you realize just how poorly formed it is! That's because you have denied yourself the chance to put that opinion out into the world, where it could interact with others and be refined, adjusted, and improved. When you decided you couldn't bear making a mistake, and you sought safety instead, you felt better in the short term, but you didn't realize that you simultaneously forfeited some positive experiences too. You could have experienced what it feels like to make a big fat mistake—and for the world not to end!

Safety-seeking behaviors are dangerous because they lure us with a false premise. We may wrongly attribute our safety measures as the cause of preventing these fears, of saving us from something we can't bear. The solution is simple but not easy: Face your fears without allowing yourself access to your safety-seeking behaviors. *Sit with* your anxiety until it subsides. Don't run from that discomfort; learn to tolerate and accept it. Here's a quick rundown of how to do that:

Step 1: Identify your safety-seeking behaviors and what you're hoping to "save" yourself from by engaging in those behaviors.

To start to tune in to some of your safety behaviors, ask yourself the following:

- When you can't avoid a situation, what do you do to make yourself feel less anxious?
- When you feel anxious in a social situation, what do you do to avoid attention?

- When you feel anxious in a social situation, what do you do to come across better to others?
- Are there situations that you have approached lots of times but that you are still anxious about? What do you do in this situation to reduce your anxiety?

For example, you might notice that you tend to mindlessly scroll through your phone or plug in some earphones in social situations to avoid having to think of something to say to people around you and having them judge you because you can't come up with anything interesting or witty to say. Or perhaps you notice that you tend to make corny jokes to prevent the conversation from evolving in certain directions, where you might be out of your depth. You notice that your safety-seeking behavior is a diversion tactic to save you from being put on the spot and expected to say something intelligent.

Step 2: Plan an experiment where you will deliberately drop one or more of your safety behaviors. What are you worried will happen if you don't do this behavior? Carefully note down what might happen if you just sat with rather than tried to escape that discomfort. Plan ahead of time how you're going to observe the results of this experiment. If you're used to keeping quiet in groups, and you challenge yourself to see what happens when you speak up, try also to notice what happens when you do. Are people really as bored, uninterested, or hostile as you imagined they'd be? Ask yourself what evidence might suggest that you were right to fear speaking up—for example, people would tell you to keep quiet, ignore you, or insult you. Remind yourself to actively look for any of these behaviors. Do people really behave as you thought they might?

Step 3: Run the experiment; analyze your data.

Take note of what actually happened when you went against your safety-seeking behavior. Perhaps you spoke up in a meeting or left your earphones at home deliberately. Maybe it was scary and uncomfortable at first, but you quickly noticed that people were usually kind or, at worst, just neutral. Take the time to notice that you *can* be okay with situations you've previously found difficult. Look at how you coped and become curious about how you might do more of that. Consider your beliefs about yourself and the situation and see if they might need adjustment. Don't forget to celebrate as well! Facing your fears takes courage, but isn't it great to see concrete evidence that you can do it? Give praise where it's due, and see what experiment you'd like to commit to next. Maybe next time you speak up in a group, you want to try sharing an opinion you know is not so popular—how will *that* feel?

Safety-seeking behaviors are a subtle kind of avoidance. They help you feel safe in the short term, but only maintain your anxiety in the long run. Your safety-seeking behaviors will be unique to you, so it's worth taking the time to pay attention to exactly what you do to reduce anxiety, and how you could choose healthier approaches. If you'd feel anxious without it, the behavior is probably safety-seeking. Dropping this habit may increase anxiety in the short term, but it will free you from your fears in the long run.

Social Exhaustion

Imagine two of your old-school friends are coming to your town, and you're meeting up after not seeing them for months. You miss them both and love spending time with them—they're your oldest and closest friends. A week in advance, you start planning their visit and all the fun stuff you'll do together when they arrive over the weekend. You're genuinely excited, but somehow, when Friday rolls around, you're feeling the tiniest bit of dread . . .

It's been a long, long week at work and you're frankly tired. You go ahead with the plans but find yourself almost forcing a smile, almost pretending that you're having more fun than you really are. And as the visit wears on, you get more and more anxious and annoyed. By the end of the evening, you're just wishing everyone would go away and leave you alone.

Because you're tired and grumpy, you're not quite as charming a conversationalist as you can be, and end up saying a few awkward things . . . then feeling more awkward. You get a little quiet, and others pick up on it. Somehow, chatting gradually feels like a grind, and soon it's clear that nobody is really enjoying themselves. By the time your friends leave at the end of the weekend, you're pretty exhausted, your mood is dark, and you find yourself dwelling on all the irritating faults and flaws in them that you never quite noticed before.

You think to yourself, "I'm just so awkward and socially anxious. I'm such an introvert, and people are such a headache. Why bother when it's so much hassle to socialize?"

You completely forget that these are your friends, that you were looking forward to seeing them, and that ordinarily you love hanging out with them. So what happened? The truth is you might not be socially anxious or introverted at all—you might just have been trying to socialize when your social battery was depleted.

Social exhaustion isn't an officially recognized condition by the American Psychological Association (APA), but it's a concept that will instantly resonate with many people. Social exhaustion generally refers to feeling drained and overstimulated after spending time with others. It can manifest differently for each individual depending on their level of extroversion or introversion, and may vary across life stages.

Signs of social exhaustion include increased irritability, escalating impatience, and a lack of joy in social engagements that were previously enjoyable. Sound familiar? The reason we'll explore social exhaustion here is that its "symptoms" often mimic those of social anxiety—but its treatment couldn't be more different.

Ater a few years of Covid lockdowns and with many of us awkwardly re-emerging into the workplace after working from home, social exhaustion has been easier to notice than ever before. Work chitchat, meetings, and social events with colleagues that previously seemed manageable suddenly seem overwhelming. The consequences may not always be obvious while at work, either. People may experience social exhaustion during office hours or when engaging in social activities outside of work, feeling like they no longer get the same satisfaction from those interactions as they once did. For some, social exhaustion is confusing because they genuinely crave social interaction on one hand, but feel drained and annoyed when it happens.

What can be done?

First of all, **recognize the difference between fearing social interactions and finding them awkward/uncomfortable versus being socially exhausted.** In the same way you wouldn't say you were unfit just because you needed to take a break after a heavy workout, it doesn't make sense to say that you lack social skills because you find socializing difficult *after you've done a lot of it*. What's more, if you're consciously trying to develop objectively weak social skills, you may be pushing yourself far out of your comfort zone and socializing more than you're used to—and this is tiring. Recognize it as tiring and give yourself appropriate time to recharge and regenerate.

When our social skills are poorly developed, when we are introverted, or when we have social anxiety that tends to make us withdraw from people, we are not just missing out on opportunities to strengthen those skills. We are also missing out on another, invisible skill set—the ability to manage our energy levels, to take breaks, to practice self-care, and to have appropriate boundaries around our time and resources. The irony is that the extroverted social butterfly may actually be better than the shy introvert when it comes to budgeting their energy and time.

Overextending yourself and becoming exhausted is a real risk for introverts or previously socially anxious people precisely because they don't have much practice in negotiating their upper bound of social interaction—they are usually too busy fixing the problem of *too little* social interaction to ever have to learn to manage *too much*! Add in the fact that introverts have often had a lifetime of people telling them to constantly cheer up and be more extroverted, that they fail to recognize that it's perfectly possible to turn down social interaction for reasons other than anxiety!

Here are some ways to start being mindful of your own limitations and working with them.

Be Clear About Your Boundaries

Sometimes you need to challenge yourself and not give your excuses and fears too much credit. But occasionally, you'll need to know where your limits are and be the first one to respect and honor them. For example, someone might be tackling social anxiety, but also genuinely does not enjoy going to bars or drinking heavily. By carefully separating their own values and boundaries from their fears, they can confidently know when to push themselves to be more social (for example, joining that interesting pottery group) and when to say no (for example, when pressured to drink too much by a crowd that cannot envision a social event that doesn't include alcohol).

In a similar vein, find your assertiveness and be okay with telling others when you're tired and ready to call a social event to a close. If you want to go home, that's okay. If you feel that hanging out with the same group of people four times a week is way too much, say so. When you can confidently express your boundaries without making it anyone's fault, you teach other people to respect those limits, too. In fact, you'd be surprised how many people will appreciate the honesty—and maybe even start being more candid with you in return.

Plan Ahead

Think of your social energy tank like a literal fuel tank in a car. You wouldn't plan a week of driving out into the middle of nowhere with only a half tank without thinking about when and where you'd refuel. Yet sometimes people plan social events in this way, without leaving enough time and space to recharge themselves afterward.

Leave yourself enough "nothing time" before and after, when you can just decompress and do nothing. Zone out in front of the TV, putter around the house, or take a nap. Try not to plan too many demanding things in a row. Social exhaustion is not the same as physical exhaustion—the only way you can really rest socially is to be on your own. That means that even being around people you live with can be too much—try to take an hour to yourself in nature, leave the house, or lock the bathroom door and have a relaxing bath where you can tune everyone out.

During the event, avoid trying to "white knuckle" things—take frequent breaks and give yourself permission to take it easy. Isn't it strange how often socially anxious people hold themselves responsible for everyone having a good time, or assume that they have to be energized and exciting and entertaining? Let yourself off the hook. Make your only goal to be yourself and to engage with others. There is no report card at the end!

Think in terms of quality and not quantity. It's much healthier (and easier!) to focus your efforts and make genuine connections with people, rather than counting the number of events you attend or tallying up the number of hours you spent doing this or not. Perhaps it's a hangover from school days where popularity was just about the sheer number of friends you had, but there really is no reason to have some arbitrary idea of how often you "should" be out every evening, or how many friends you should have. It's about how well you engage with those people.

Give yourself time and practice self-compassion. If you're overcoming some social anxiety, it will feel scary at first. It helps to have realistic expectations of yourself and to not be too quick to beat yourself up if you're not moving as fast as you believe you should be (there's that pesky word again—*should*!). Try not to compare yourself to anyone else.

Recognize the signs that your tank is getting empty, and be ready to step back and recharge. This is your responsibility—there's no point pushing yourself and then getting annoyed with other people for making demands on you. If you notice yourself getting cranky, unfocused, or bored, just gracefully find a way to end the interaction. With socializing, there's a wisdom in "quitting while you're ahead."

Don't be afraid to reevaluate certain relationships or situations. Do you have someone who frequently guilts you or shames you or pressures you to do things you're not really comfortable doing? Are you in a job where it's difficult to take care of your own health and well-being? Are you carrying too much of the social burden in your relationship, or are you caught in a toxic family situation? Be kind to yourself and make those necessary changes to start creating a healthier, more balanced social life.

Summary:

- Action is important: Being sociable, confident, calm, and capable is not something you feel; it's something you do. We ultimately learn to be better at socializing by socializing—not by thinking, planning, imagining, or hoping. That's why it's important to put limits around your rumination and constantly remind yourself that you cannot overthink your way out of overthinking. Understand that chronic worry and rumination are not an excess of thinking, but a deficit of meaningful action.
- Worrying occasionally is human; accept it and let it go. Be mindful of your thoughts and feelings and realize that you don't necessarily have to get on board with every passing thought that comes your way. If you must worry, do it on your own terms by scheduling deliberate "worry time" and noticing what happens. Try to discharge anxiety into the environment by challenging it into intelligent action. Ask "what can I DO to clear and release this anxiety?"

Sometimes you need to mine an experience for meaning in order to learn a lesson and finally move on.
- Exposure therapy is a classic cognitive behavioral approach and is essentially an attempt to break down negative associations and conditioned responses and set up conditions where new ones can be formed. If anxiety has been learned, that means it can be unlearned. Face your feared situation and avoid escaping until your conditioned anxiety response fades.
- Graded exposure entails identifying your fear, breaking it down into a hierarchy of increasingly challenging tasks, then attempting each task starting from the easiest. As you go, you experience your anxiety and practice relaxation until your automatic fear response is weakened and disappears. It's important to be aware of and let go of safety-seeking behaviors. Find the healthy balance between comfort and challenge.
- Social anxiety sometimes means we're less adept at recognizing and correcting social exhaustion when it happens. Take breaks, plan ahead, assert your boundaries, and budget your energy

and resources so you have enough time to recuperate and recharge.

Chapter Five: Developing Relaxed Communication

When you're socially anxious, it seems for the longest time that your only goal is to socialize without being anxious! This really is the case, but once you've started to better self-regulate and engage with people with curiosity instead of fear, you may realize that this is really just the first step. It's a little like overcoming the fear of flying—once you start to get comfortable, you may have an "aha!" moment when it suddenly dawns on you just how amazing flying is. You can go anywhere in the world . . .

The point of learning to be more comfortable, natural, and confident with others is not so you can adjust yourself to some external standard or learn to endure something genuinely unpleasant. **Rather, learning to**

socialize comfortably is about opening yourself up to the amazing world of opportunity that lies within human connection. When you leave behind your fear, you have the option to feel so many other things—interest, curiosity, excitement, joy, connection, love, appreciation, pride, comfort . . . The list is endless.

As you master both yourself and the way you interact with others, remind yourself of what is on the other side of your limiting fears.

Bulletproof Conversation Skills

The first step is usually the hardest. This is definitely true of conversation. Luckily, you can easily learn to use "conversation openers" to help you quickly navigate those potentially awkward first moments.

Chatting with someone from a "cold start" can be initially challenging, but try to reframe this feeling as only a mild, inevitable hesitation. Everyone feels it to some extent, but it's no reason to hold back or doubt yourself. Starting conversations is just a skill and habit like any other—the more you do it, the more familiar it will become and the easier it will get.

Here's a basic method for breezing through the opening of a conversation:

- Prepare by choosing a conversation starter
- Actively imagine and anticipate positive responses and outcomes
- Keep relaxing yourself with deep breaths and positive self-talk

Think of your conversation starter as a bullet loaded in a gun. It should be ready to go at the slightest squeeze of the trigger. It can be nerve-wracking to take that first step, but the more prepared you are, the less you have to do to trigger off a chain of events. Yes, it *will* feel uncomfortable and scary at first—but your goal is not to do things perfectly on the first try, but to just make that first try so the second one is a little bit easier, and the third one easier still. Expect that it will take practice.

A big part of what makes initial encounters so anxiety-provoking is not the encounters themselves, but rather all the expectations and beliefs we bring to them. If we expect to be rejected or judged, or anticipate that we'll be uncomfortable, we enter the interaction in a fearful, guarded state. Often, our fears become self-fulfilling prophecies.

"Mental rehearsal" is a way to use the power of the self-fulfilling prophesy to your own advantage. You can actively expect and anticipate positive things—and this will influence everything in the right direction, creating a positive feedback loop. To break the vicious cycle of self-doubt and fear, we need to stop expecting the worst, and start expecting the best. As you become desensitized to all those things that used to scare you, it's as though you're gathering more and more evidence that your previous beliefs are plain wrong, and teaching yourself a new lesson: Meeting new people is really no big deal and can actually be kind of fun! Not only can you do it, you can even enjoy it.

For those with moderate-to-severe social anxiety, forcing themselves to initiate conversations may not be the most effective approach. Instead, the method introduces a more practical and easier way to gain social confidence. Planning what to say in conversations involves spending a week going to familiar places and observing people while taking notes. The primary goal during this observation period is to gather information without actively engaging in conversations.

Practice Engaging with the World
Bearing in mind that anxiety narrows our focus and forces our attention inward, try this exercise to keep your mind on the external world, not in a state of fear but in a state of gentle curiosity and awareness. Try this:

Step 1: Observe

For a week, just spend some time in "observation mode." Go to places where you or other people hang out, and just sit quietly and notice everything around you. It'll be easier to do this when you are calm and on your own, but eventually, the goal is to maintain this curious, open-minded attitude while you're engaging with others.

Take a look at your surroundings and how people are behaving. Ask yourself questions about what's happening, unspoken details, emotions, and the intricacies of the environment.

- What is happening around me?
- What is one thing that's obvious but nobody is speaking about?
- What is a specific person doing, and what is his/her purpose being out here?
- What are the facial expressions of the people around me expressing?
- What emotions are on their face? What might they be thinking?
- What are people wearing? Anything unusual? Are they trying to communicate something?
- What is obvious about the environment? What stands out?

You could even note your answers in a notebook, if you like, and look for patterns. Next, look at these observations and try to turn them into statements or questions. For example,

"I like that lamp."

"That plant needs water."

"The sun really lights up this room."

"The countertop is so messy."

"I wonder where he's from?"

"I wonder what she's doing for work?"

"Is she nervous or is that how she always looks?"

Now what you have is a list of tiny topics—the beginnings of a conversation. Practice in a few different locations to get the hang of this and then move on to the next step.

Step 2: Turn observations into starters and stories

The only reason human beings created language was because they desperately wanted to share something of their world with one another. This is where you'll begin when creating your own conversation starters! Review your notes at home and use the gathered information to create good conversation starters based on what you observed, heard, or sensed during your interactions.

For example, during one of your observations, you noticed a person wearing a unique T-shirt with the logo of your favorite band. The next time you see someone wearing a band T-shirt, you can start the conversation with: "Hey, I couldn't help but notice your T-shirt! I'm a huge fan of [band name]. Have you seen them live before?" And just like that, you've started a conversation. From here, you can tell a story about your concert experience when you saw that band.

This technique works so well because it teaches you how to start conversations in the way they already naturally occur. Think about the *worst* way that people open conversations—lame pickup lines. These often fail not because they're not witty enough, but because they are very obviously rehearsed and usually have no real connection to the real moment or the environment. They're unnatural, and it's *this* that makes them feel awkward. But if you create conversation openers using the above technique, you'll find you're a lot less nervous to strike up a conversation with someone, because it will seem more organic and natural to do so—you are just spontaneously engaging with the environment, and this is spurring you to share something with them.

Approaching conversations from a place of fear and desperation only makes them harder. Approach instead with a playful, relaxed, and genuine desire to connect with someone in a natural way, and everything becomes much, much easier. **The trick is to continually turn outward and engage.** If you are caught up in your head and agonizing over fears that are completely disconnected from the concrete situation you're in, you are not really connected to your environment—and that makes it harder to connect to a big part of that environment, which is other people.

Now, a big caveat here is that although it's worth doing this exercise and practicing being more aware of your surroundings, you don't want to literally rehearse conversation openers. With just a small amount of practice, this is something you can easily learn to do in the moment. In fact, you might find it useful to get into the habit of "blurting." Don't overthink things, just express. Don't sit and think to yourself about what you plan to say, because to do so would mean turning inward. Just say the first thing that pops into your mind. Really! Don't be afraid to express your initial emotional reaction to something—even a facial expression can communicate so much and make an instant connection with someone.

The truth is that starting conversations is not difficult, and it doesn't take much. Remind yourself that you are not performing on a stage, you are not a salesperson trying to convince someone of something (your worth, maybe?), and you're not making unreasonable or unusual demands of anyone. One final tip for making it easier to break the ice initially is to imagine that the person you're about to talk to already is your friend, and that you've already been introduced and are perfectly comfortable with one another. **How would you behave in the presence of someone you knew well but were just seeing for the first time that day?** Try to do the same when meeting someone new.

Try Improv

Whatever the exact flavor of your overthinking, and no matter how social anxiety manifests for you, the solution is usually the same: **Get out of your head and get into the moment**. Rather than churning uselessly in your own mind over thoughts and feelings that are distorted and disconnected from the world, unplug that inner chatter machine called your mind and plug yourself into the real, unfolding moment around you.

Though doing any kind of public speaking or performance may make most socially anxious people break out into a cold sweat, there's good reason to forego therapy and sign up for an improv class instead. In improv, there's just no time for overthinking. The whole premise only works if you are externalizing, taking action, and flowing with the moment. The goal, of course, is not to become really good at improv (although don't assume that that's an impossibility if you're a shy or anxious person!) but to take the lessons you learn on the improv stage and bring them into your everyday life.

There's no point in lying: **You totally *will* feel silly at first, and there are definitely going to be some awkward moments. But after that, something interesting happens.** You realize that it's not the end of the world to have to think on your feet and to not always know exactly how a social situation will pan out. Think of it as exposure therapy, where your irrational fear is of uncertainty and ambiguity itself. The more you expose yourself to these things without escaping, the more you see that not only are they not threatening, they can actually be really good fun.

This is the secret: The opposite of anxiety is not calm and relaxation. It's excitement. It's engagement, joy, energy, vivacity, authenticity, playfulness, curiosity, expression, spontaneity—it's life.

A study led by Peter Felsman highlights the significance of improv as a serious social and emotional tool. The study involved Detroit students participating in a ten-week improv course conducted by The Improv Project. Surveys were given to students at the beginning and end of the program to measure uncertainty intolerance, social anxiety, and social efficacy.

The hypothesis was that improv training would lower social anxiety and uncertainty intolerance, and these two factors were correlated. To put it really simply, improv involves dealing with uncertainty, as participants have to adapt to their partner's spontaneous actions. Felsman's team had previously published an experimental paper in 2020, demonstrating that improv led to increased uncertainty tolerance. The new study aimed to explore whether improv's link to reduced social anxiety could be explained by its impact on uncertainty intolerance.

The findings revealed that **after ten weeks of improv, there was a significant decrease in**

overall social anxiety and uncertainty intolerance in the group. Moreover, students diagnosed with social anxiety showed even more substantial reductions in these areas. Active participation in the improv workshops led to more significant decreases in uncertainty intolerance and social anxiety. The study also found a correlation between changes in uncertainty intolerance and changes in social anxiety.

Feldman suggests that **uncertainty is inevitable in life, and we have two options: plan for it or learn to tolerate it**. If you're an anxious overthinker, you're already more than familiar with the first strategy—and what it costs in the long run. It's possible, too, that Feldman's conclusions were a little conservative and that there is a third option when faced with uncertainty: relish it. Some of the most brilliant comedy, the juiciest banter, the most engaging conversations, and the sweetest moments of "chemistry" come down to people not just tolerating uncertainty but learning to dance and play with it.

The study shows us that exposure to uncertainty in a supportive improv environment can increase comfort with uncertainty and subsequently reduce social anxiety. What's great about it is that this is never done in a dry, hypothetical way—you are not sitting in a therapist's chair, talking about what you are afraid of or what you might do tomorrow. You are fully there, in the moment, engaging dynamically with your environment. And every moment you spend doing that, you are teaching yourself invaluable skills of emotional regulation, confidence, self-trust, curiosity, and exactly the kind of open and flowing spirit that makes socializing a breeze.

If you've never done improv before or have any idea of what it's about, it's simple: Improv is a form of live theater where all the action and dialogue are made up spontaneously, on the spot. People love improv because it's an advanced form of make-believe and play; it's a way to loosen up, have fun, and get over yourself! It's not scripted or polished—in other words, it's the perfect place to practice getting really good at being in the moment. Here are some improv-inspired principles that you can apply to your own life right now if you're not ready to sign up for a class just yet:

Find the Game
In improv there is a concept called "finding the game." What it means is that improvisers pay special attention to fun patterns as they pop up so they can keep them going. Overthinkers, in their own way, do the same thing, but

instead of looking for the fun, they tend to unconsciously seek out all those little observations that they can pounce on and use as confirmation of their catastrophic, worst-case predictions for an interaction.

Instead of overthinking and getting anxious, focus on finding the fun or "the game" in a situation. Home in on everything that seems a little silly. Be on the lookout for something mildly amusing, nonsensical, or strange. Then, instead of focusing your attention on internal negative feelings and interpretations, amplify these fleeting moments of whimsy. Look for details you can play around with and have fun with, shifting your focus externally.

For example, in the "Alien Game," the person uses their imagination to pretend they are an alien trying to blend in with Earthlings, which helps them find patterns in their behavior and reduces overthinking. The objective is not necessarily to find this game, but rather to cultivate the kind of mindset that is always open and receptive to the possibility of something new and interesting emerging—with your help. When you shift focus and tap into a childlike sense of curiosity, you can't help but lower your anxiety. It's pretty obvious: Fear and play are mutually exclusive, and it's impossible to feel anxious while feeling curious at the same time. Focus on one and you cannot be the other.

Treat Others like Geniuses

Being socially anxious comes with an unspoken fearful belief that we are not only constantly being watched, but that people are also appraising us and inevitably finding us deficient. One of the pioneers for improv, Del Close, once said that if we can treat our fellow improvisers like geniuses, poets, and talented artists, they'll actually be more able to become that on stage. Having trust in other people's powers of spontaneity has surprisingly quick effects—and the same holds true when you trust *yourself* in this way.

This is a radical shift from the anxious mindset that tells us that other people are always to be regarded first as a threat, that they may be harsh strangers who will judge or reject us. Instead, when we respect people and how they want to steer an interaction, when we become genuinely curious about their completely unique perspective, and when we respond to their contributions with authentic interest and gratitude, we find that any interaction becomes elevated. This is the realm where people forget themselves and their fears, abandon their plans and expectations, and submit to the flow ... and then magic happens.

Find the game, and in the same way try to find the best in other people. Start from a position where you are automatically assuming that other people are kind, interesting, entertaining, wise, and fun—you are just in the process of discovering how. Playing the "Superhero Game" involves figuring out what someone's superhero identity is. For instance, if you meet someone who is very warm, you can call them Super Friendly Girl, even if just in your own mind. Engage with them where their warmth is put front and center.

When someone shares an opinion or idea with you, imagine that your entire being pauses and turns all its attention to what they're sharing, and take their expression as though it were a gift, genuinely considering it in good faith even if at first it seems wrong or alien to you. Experiment and, just for a moment, **treat other people as though they are the most interesting, most important person in the world**. You'd be amazed at how people "blossom" in your presence when you can do this . . . and how quickly it allows you to drop your own anxieties and fears.

Yes, and . . .
This is probably one of the first things most people learn when attempting improv. The concept is simple: **No matter what the other improvisers do or say, and no matter which**

direction they steer the situation in, your only job is to affirm and elaborate. The idea is to never negate the "move" the other improvers make, but pick it up and run with it. They have suddenly turned the entire encounter into a comedic misunderstanding? Okay. Go with that! They're speaking German now? Okay. Sure. What happens next?

When we're anxious we tend to be fixed, even stubborn, in our thinking. We have an idea about how we want things to unfold, or how we feel they *should* unfold, and we hold on to it so tightly that the interaction cannot unfold spontaneously. Because we keep pulling things back to some unspoken agenda, the conversation is stifled and unnatural. To put this another way, fear is boring! The more anxious we are and the more unwilling we are to embrace uncertainty, the more we plan and the less relaxed and free our expression becomes. There's just nothing to be surprised by (can you imagine how impossible it is to find something humorous or charming if you're unwilling to relinquish control and be surprised?).

Practice the "Yes, and" rule by being more open-minded and willing to explore ideas, especially when you tend to default to saying no. You'll build effective communication and a spirit of collaboration, helping curb your social anxiety. In real-life scenarios, use "Yes, and" to acknowledge the other person's perspective without necessarily agreeing with it, fostering a deeper understanding and strengthening relationships.

This mindset shift helps you believe that no possible outcome is really worth getting anxious about. It's okay if you don't know what you're going to say next—and the more you place yourself in that situation, the more you'll see that uncertainty can even be fun rather than anxiety-provoking. You can trust your conversation partner to lead and steer the direction of conversation—who knows, maybe it will be interesting? There's only one way to find out!

In 2008 lead researcher Charles Limb did fMRI scans on both improv performers and jazz musicians who were improvising. He discovered that people who were improvising had brain activity markedly different from people who were engaging in more predictable, planned activities (in other words, acting from a script or playing from sheet music).

When people improvise, there is reduced activity in the dorsolateral prefrontal cortex, which is the part of the brain that, loosely, we can associate with the "inner critic." Whenever you hear that negative inner voice that tells you "Oh my God, don't say that," it's associated with activity in this region of the brain. It's the part of the brain that wants to say "no, but" rather than "yes, and." The medial prefrontal cortex, on the other hand, is more connected with language and creativity, and this tends to show greater activity during improvising. So, when you improvise, you are essentially quieting down your inner critic while cultivating a more creative, playful, and open-minded way of being. Being in this state of mind doesn't mean you never make mistakes, but it does mean you no longer see little gaffes and blunders as mistakes at all—rather, they are magically transformed into *comedy*, and they, too, are welcome and allowed to unfold as a welcome part of the game.

The next time you're in any social interaction, imagine that you're in an improv class. Think of it as a game. **See your conversation partners as much valued fellow co-creators, and imagine that you are excited about what you are discovering together (which doesn't exist yet!) rather than anxious about whether you're doing a good job or not.** Finding the game, appreciating other people, and being open-minded to whatever emerges in the conversation—these are three subtle but incredibly powerful ways to shift out of anxiety mode. Socializing doesn't have to be a trial to endure, but something genuinely enjoyable.

With mindful intention, positive expectation, and a willingness to just play and see what happens, you become a better listener, a self-possessed and confident speaker, and a lot more charismatic, too.

Mastering Assertive Communication

In our final chapter, we're going to explore what might be a less frequently discussed consequence of social anxiety—a lack of assertiveness. Consider this all-too-common situation: Someone was really rude to you at work during lunch and said something wholly inappropriate. In the moment, you were a little stunned and hurt, but you said nothing. Then the moment passed. Later that evening, you're at home and stewing over it (hello, post-event rumination!) and thinking of all the clever things you should have said when you had the chance.

Perhaps your lack of assertiveness shows up in other ways. There may be someone in your life who repeatedly takes advantage, pushes your boundaries, or makes unreasonable demands on you that you never quite feel able to decline. Perhaps you are constantly regretting not "speaking up" when you knew something was wrong, or you feel passed over in the workplace because you bite your tongue or hang back . . . and then you watch as someone else happily steps in and takes the opportunity that could have been yours.

Many individuals, including those with social anxiety, struggle with assertiveness due to fears of being seen as pushy or argumentative. People with social anxiety often adopt a passive communication style to avoid conflict, but this can hinder expressing their needs and desires. If you are constantly tangled up with your own internal anxieties and worries, it usually means that you're less available to respond naturally and spontaneously to opportunities and threats as they unfold in your environment. You may fail to capitalize on a positive opportunity because you're overthinking, and you fail to defend yourself against a boundary infringement for the same reason.

For example, someone mistreats us, and we get trapped in our heads, stewing over who is really to blame and how to interpret this or that action and what it all means. We may end up wracked with guilt or shame or resentment about what "should" have happened, all the while failing to take the action required to defend our boundaries—for example, making sure that we don't continue to allow that person to mistreat us.

The overthinker is someone who will stay up all night rehearsing exactly how they are going to have a difficult conversation with someone in the morning; a non-anxious person will simply raise their objections in the very moment they occur so that the entire issue is resolved immediately, and they sleep soundly that same night. We may be so busy overthinking what someone else thinks of us that we never really stop to ask what *we* think of *them* . . . and in the process allow them to walk all over us!

If you're reading this book, chances are you want to develop all those positive social skills, such as winning friends, building charisma, communicating well, learning to speak in public, and so on. But there are other social skills we tend to forget: knowing how to say no, to complain, to assert a boundary, to state our opinion, to claim what we're entitled to, or to defend ourselves against insult and injury. **Being a better socializer doesn't just mean learning the rules of friendliness—it also means learning to stand up for yourself and, if necessary, manage conflict.**

Unfortunately, for many of us our low self-esteem, shyness, and lack of assertiveness all combine to create an overall passive pattern of interaction that usually leaves us feeling more and more disempowered. We might be reluctant to communicate how we really feel because, when it comes down to it, we're afraid:

"If I assert myself, I'm *afraid* that . . .

. . . people will be overwhelmed or inconvenienced

. . . people will judge or reject me

. . . people will stop loving me

. . . people will think I'm rude or aggressive

. . . people will think I'm weird/uptight/demanding."

In the same way that socially anxious people can misunderstand what being "sociable" actually means, they can misunderstand what being "assertive" is—assertiveness is not aggressiveness toward others, it's not being unreasonable, fussy, or rude, and it's not about forcing or coercing others to do what we want. Rather, it's an offshoot of confidence: the ability to own ourselves and our experiences, to take up space, to expect what we are entitled to, and to carry ourselves with a certain degree of non-negotiable confidence, composure, and self-respect. So really, assertiveness has nothing at all to do with other people's behavior, and everything to do with our own—what we think and feel, the limits we set for ourselves, and how we communicate those to other people.

For socially anxious people, the fear of rejection can be disproportionate and get in the way of them standing up for themselves or claiming their rights. Some anxious people may be too passive, allowing themselves to be dominated by others, but then violently swing to the other extreme, becoming overly aggressive when everything becomes too much. Healthy assertiveness is somewhere in the middle: We assert our rights while respecting the rights of others; we value our own perspective while acknowledging the other persons.

Assertiveness lies between passive and aggressive communication styles, involving open and direct expression of opinions and needs while recognizing others. It emphasizes owning and taking responsibility for one's thoughts and opinions. This means not allowing others to bully or dominate you, but it also means not expecting others to take responsibility for you or waiting for others to give you permission to take action.

Often, socially anxious people can find themselves trapped in people-pleasing behaviors and unable to speak up for themselves. The irony is that just a little clear, assertive communication early on can save you from years of misunderstanding, obligation, guilt, shame, poor communication, and resentment later down the line. In other words, learning to be more assertive actually means you live with *fewer* confrontations and conflicts, not more!

Here are the three concrete ways to become more assertive in everyday life, even if you're socially anxious:

Use "I" Statements

By forcing yourself to speak in first person, you teach yourself to get comfortable expressing your thoughts and feelings directly. Keep it simple: Start with "I," then add a verb that describes what you are feeling (like, dislike, want, need, feel, love, hate, wish . . .). Finish the sentence to describe what it is that you are feeling:

"I wish you would spend more time with me."

"I feel lonely."

"I don't like unexpected guests."

That said, being assertive doesn't just mean correcting or berating others or raising a complaint. The following statements, for example, are also assertive:

"I really enjoyed our conversation today."

"I know you're not a fan, but I love old romance novels!"

"I'm not sure how I feel about that. Can I have some time to think things over?"

Not only is "I" talk generally a good communication habit, it will help you make sure that you're keeping your message pure and clear without resorting to blame or demands.

Keep Your Emotions under Control
You don't have to be angry, upset, or indignant to communicate assertively or protect a boundary. In fact, avoid getting overly emotional or attacking others when expressing yourself. Stick to describing your feelings and needs neutrally and without blaming or berating anyone else. Remember that you are not dictating what others should do; you're explaining how you feel and what you will do in certain conditions. See the difference:

"You come over unannounced and it stresses me out."

"I don't like unexpected guests."

You always have a right to your own preferences, needs, and limits. Of course, you don't have a right to control what *other* people's preferences, needs, or limits are. Maintain a positive and constructive tone to your communication, be proactive, and take responsibility for your own position. This keeps the focus where it belongs: on you and the message you're trying to assert.

Closely connected to this is the ability to disagree without it being a problem. Confident people do not see difference as a potential threat or something they need to apologize for or fix. Unconfident people feel unable to share their own opinion if it's not popular, and they're insecure in their own authentic identity. Practice saying what you really think and feel without explanation, justification, or apology. Hear other people's different opinions and simply don't react to them, either. Realize that two people can have a great conversation even if they don't agree; it's not necessary for either to win or convince anyone of anything.

Watch Your Nonverbal Behavior
In addition to what you say, pay attention to your nonverbal communication. **Stand up straight, maintain good eye contact, and**

speak with a strong, relaxed voice. Avoid fidgeting, looking down, or using aggressive body language. Avoid acting like you are doing something extremely risky and unusual by speaking your mind. For example, you don't need to give a dozen excuses for why you can't do something, apologize three times, beg forgiveness, and then suggest several ways you can "make it up" to them. Instead, just be polite, say you're not available, and move on swiftly. You will find that the more you respect your own assertions, the more others will. Take yourself seriously, and others will eventually have to do the same!

Likewise, avoid "saying" two different things at once. If you are saying "no" but your body language is really saying "no?" then you are diluting your message. If you share a limit and then willfully push beyond your own limit when pressured, you are sending mixed messages. Instead, assert yourself with the belief and expectation that others will hear and respect what you are sharing.

Guilt, shame, and fear of hurting people's feelings are usually serious concerns, but realize that none of these things are required for you to be an assertive communicator. If you are polite, then someone else's disappointment or negative reaction to your reasonable boundary is something *they* are choosing—it is not something you have inflicted on them. If you are respectfully and reasonably expressing your own needs and limits (which are just as valid as everybody else's), then someone else's choice to react negatively to that is their problem to solve, not yours.

Try to remind yourself that others are no more special or important than you are, and that you never have to undermine yourself in order to keep others happy. When we are coming from a place of anxiety, we can slip into a "bargaining" mindset where we act in an unconscious attempt to offset what we're afraid of; for example, you worry that if you assert yourself, people will withdraw their love, and so you strike an unspoken bargain that you will continue to keep quiet and ignore your needs and limits in return for them continuing to treat you well. But healthy relationships are about respectful negotiation between both people's reasonable demands—and usually the socially anxious person is in the habit of not expressing their needs *enough*, rather than expressing them too much or too forcefully.

Summary:

- Learning to socialize comfortably is about opening yourself up to the amazing world of opportunity that lies within human connection. A great social skill to develop is the ability to create conversation starters. Learn to be curious about your environment, and transform your observations into questions or comments you can share with people, actively imagine and anticipate a positive response from them, and continually maintain relaxation and positive self-talk as you stay with those awkward first moments.

- Keep turning outward, keep engaged, and stay curious and playful. Signing up for improv classes is a great way to cultivate this attitude, to get out of your head and into the moment. It will be uncomfortable at first, but the rewards are enormous. Research finds that people who do improv show a significant decrease in social anxiety and uncertainty intolerance.
- Practicing "finding the game" in social situations, and follow fun and unexpected threads. Treat others with respectful curiosity and trust their spontaneity and where they want to steer the conversation. Finally, practice the "yes, and" rule, which says that no matter what the other improvisers do

or say, your only job is to affirm and elaborate.

- Many people with social anxiety can struggle with assertiveness due to fears of being seen as pushy or argumentative, or simply because they're caught up in their own ruminations. Being a better socializer doesn't just mean learning the rules of friendliness, but also standing up for yourself and negotiating conflict.
- Try to stick to "I" statements when you express yourself, and don't get overly emotional or assign blame. Stay calm, neutral, and solutions-focused. Be mindful of your nonverbal communication, too, and make sure that your voice and body language are in alignment with your words. Stand up straight, maintain good eye contact, and speak with a strong, relaxed voice.

Summary Guide

CHAPTER ONE: INSIDE THE OVERTHINKER'S MIND

- Often a problem with socializing is really a problem with anxiety on a deeper level. Over-analyzing and rumination is common. If we solve the underlying anxiety problem, we free ourselves up to improve our social skills, just as we would any other skill.
- While anxiety narrows and restricts our attention and awareness, socializing requires we open our attention and engage more fully with our external environment.
- Social rumination is a cycle; to break it, we need to understand what maintains it. Start by admitting/accepting that your thoughts may be distorted, then separate your appraisal of reality from reality itself, and distinguish discomfort from total disaster.
- Occasional anxiety is normal; it's not dangerous or the end of the world. Embrace imperfection and vulnerability, and question whether there's any evidence for negative

assumptions, conclusions, and judgments. Your expectations may be unrealistic, your standards too high, or you may be ignoring/discounting the positive.
- The spotlight effect is a cognitive distortion where people overestimate how much others notice and care about their behavior in social situations. Try to expand your awareness so that you're not the center of things, and make your appraisals less *personal*, less *pervasive*, and less *permanent*.
- Discern between thoughts, feelings, and reality, and consciously consider alternative explanations—sometimes, it's necessary to simply tolerate ambiguity and uncertainty.
- Finally, generalization is taking a limited piece of data and extrapolating from it to situations you haven't encountered yet. With distorted thinking, overgeneralization can create anxiety. Continually seek out counterexamples of any foregone conclusions you're making, be kind to yourself, be moderate, and refuse to let isolated experiences define you completely.

CHAPTER TWO: GETTING OUT OF YOUR HEAD

- Anxiety is a problem of misdirected attention, an excessive tendency to turn inward, and a detachment from the living, dynamic environment—it's living "fifty worries behind."
- For the socially anxious, the curious state of mind is like medicine. It gets you out of your head and back into the world, where you can start acting, engaging, learning, creating, and communicating. To counter social anxiety, aim always to reconnect with the present moment.
- Practice expressing yourself more freely and spontaneously, and engage in deliberate "wonder-spotting," where you turn your curious mind out into the world and away from anxious inner rumination.
- We need to acknowledge that anxiety primes us to escape/avoid, and consciously do the opposite. Figure out how you feel and what your first impulse is, then act in the opposite way, giving yourself a chance to genuinely experience something different to see what happens.

- Progress is achieved when we learn to recognize our inner critic and gain psychological distance from it, seeing it as something you can have a fruitful conversation with. Become aware of distorted, overly critical thinking and practice curiosity without judgment: What is your inner critic trying to tell you? What is it worried will happen if you don't listen to it? Thank it for trying to help, but consciously look for healthier, more reasonable alternatives to its negative interpretation.
- Challenging distorted or critical self-talk is something you can do from a place of compassion; you can accept how you feel and look for ways to change without condemning yourself.

CHAPTER THREE: ENGAGE AGAIN

- Visualization is a great way to reconnect with the power of your own mind to create your experience. You can cultivate relaxation and emotional regulation to better cope with and counter social anxiety before, during, or after an event, or you can use your imagination to mentally rehearse in vivid detail a scenario you'd like to make more real in your life.

- A "safe space" visualization can be a way to counter a hyper-aroused autonomic nervous system so that you're able to think more clearly and calmly about a situation. Carefully imagine the place, create doorways and triggers into that memory, and then practice entering into the safe space at will. Visualization also helps you build new neural pathways in your brain and practice alternative ways of thinking, feeling, and behaving before you try it out in the real world.
- Role-playing takes visualization one step further, as we *act out* alternative ways of coping or engaging with a scenario. People with social anxiety tend to exaggerate other people's negative perceptions of them, but when they role-play being those other people, these perceptions tend to be corrected, and they feel less anxious.
- Cognitive distortions, faulty beliefs, and unhelpful attitudes all grow stronger the longer we allow them to go unchallenged. In role-play, we can artificially expose ourselves to counterevidence so these distortions

can be weakened. You can also visualize or rehearse a desired outcome, such as making believe you possess certain social skills and practicing/exploring what that would feel like.
- Finally, random acts of kindness can reduce anxiety because they challenge the fearful way we may be approaching social interactions, and create an expectation of kindness and gratitude rather than hostility. We collapse the "me versus them" framework, get out of our own heads, and focus on positive action. This state of mind is incompatible with fear and perception of threat.

CHAPTER FOUR: TAKE ACTION!

- Action is important: Being sociable, confident, calm, and capable is not something you feel; it's something you do. We ultimately learn to be better at socializing by socializing—not by thinking, planning, imagining, or hoping. That's why it's important to put limits around your rumination and constantly remind yourself that you cannot overthink your way out of overthinking. Understand that chronic worry and rumination are not an excess of thinking, but a deficit of meaningful action.

- Worrying occasionally is human; accept it and let it go. Be mindful of your thoughts and feelings and realize that you don't necessarily have to get on board with every passing thought that comes your way. If you must worry, do it on your own terms by scheduling deliberate "worry time" and noticing what happens. Try to discharge anxiety into the environment by challenging it into intelligent action. Ask "what can I DO to clear and release this anxiety?" Sometimes you need to mine an experience for meaning in order to learn a lesson and finally move on.
- Exposure therapy is a classic cognitive behavioral approach and is essentially an attempt to break down negative associations and conditioned responses and set up conditions where new ones can be formed. If anxiety has been learned, that means it can be unlearned. Face your feared situation and avoid escaping until your conditioned anxiety response fades.

- Graded exposure entails identifying your fear, breaking it down into a hierarchy of increasingly challenging tasks, then attempting each task starting from the easiest. As you go, you experience your anxiety and practice relaxation until your automatic fear response is weakened and disappears. It's important to be aware of and let go of safety-seeking behaviors. Find the healthy balance between comfort and challenge.
- Social anxiety sometimes means we're less adept at recognizing and correcting social exhaustion when it happens. Take breaks, plan ahead, assert your boundaries, and budget your energy and resources so you have enough time to recuperate and recharge.

CHAPTER FIVE: DEVELOPING RELAXED COMMUNICATION

- Learning to socialize comfortably is about opening yourself up to the amazing world of opportunity that lies within human connection. A great social skill to develop is the ability to create conversation starters. Learn to be curious about your environment, and transform your observations into questions or comments you can share with people, actively imagine and anticipate a positive response from them, and continually maintain relaxation and positive self-talk as you stay with those awkward first moments.

- Keep turning outward, keep engaged, and stay curious and playful. Signing up for improv classes is a great way to cultivate this attitude, to get out of your head and into the moment. It will be uncomfortable at first, but the rewards are enormous. Research finds that people who do improv show a significant decrease in social anxiety and uncertainty intolerance.
- Practicing "finding the game" in social situations, and follow fun and unexpected threads. Treat others with respectful curiosity and trust their spontaneity and where they want to steer the conversation. Finally, practice the "yes, and" rule, which says that no matter what the other improvisers do or say, your only job is to affirm and elaborate.

- Many people with social anxiety can struggle with assertiveness due to fears of being seen as pushy or argumentative, or simply because they're caught up in their own ruminations. Being a better socializer doesn't just mean learning the rules of friendliness, but also standing up for yourself and negotiating conflict.
- Try to stick to "I" statements when you express yourself, and don't get overly emotional or assign blame. Stay calm, neutral, and solutions-focused. Be mindful of your nonverbal communication, too, and make sure that your voice and body language are in alignment with your words. Stand up straight, maintain good eye contact, and speak with a strong, relaxed voice.